Authors:
Grace Jasmine
Julia Jasmine, M.A.

Illustrator:
Keith Vasconcelles

Editor:
Dona Herweck Rice

Art Direction:
Elayne Roberts

Cover Artist:
Sue Fullam

Imaging:
Rick Chacón

Publishers:
Rachelle Cracchiolo, M.S. Ed.
Mary Dupuy Smith, M.S. Ed.

Cooperative Learning Activities for Language Arts

Teacher Created Materials, Inc.
P.O. Box 1040
Huntington Beach, CA 92647
©1994 Teacher Created Materials, Inc.
Made in U.S.A.

ISBN-1-55734-650-X

Table of Contents

Introduction

Welcome to the wonderful world of cooperative learning! This book is designed to help primary students learn language arts skills while actively engaged in cooperative activities based on the general theme of land, sea, and air travel.

A Complete Resource Book

This book provides everything you need to present a language arts unit using cooperative learning activities. It includes not only innovative ideas but also practical suggestions and blackline masters to help you put the ideas into action in your classroom.

The first sections explain how to make cooperative learning a part of your curriculum. They include an overview, instructions and activities for introducing cooperative learning to your students and parents, guidelines for setting up groups, ideas for activity centers, and suggestions for assessment and portfolios.

The rest of the book provides a wide range of cooperative activities divided into three parts.

Cooperation by Land centers around the various forms of land travel. Children will examine the sights and sounds of traveling by car, express their ideas about bicycle safety, read about railroads, and write about a fantasy bus trip.

Cooperation by Sea centers around the ocean. Children will hunt for treasure, experience underwater adventures, go fishing, and even take care of a live goldfish. This unit is set up so no matter where you live, experiencing the sea will be easy and fun!

Cooperation by Air centers around air travel and the writing process. This section of the book divides the writing process into separate cooperative activities. You may focus on the activities that are relevant for your classroom or use the unit in sequential order to present the complete writing process in a unique way.

Easy to Use

This book is designed with the busy teacher in mind. Each activity unit includes a complete lesson plan which explains the **purpose** of the unit, the **skills** to be taught, and the **materials** that are needed.

The **procedures** for teaching the unit are described in detail. Ways **to simplify** the unit are provided. These suggestions allow you to adapt the activity to the pre-cooperative learners in a classroom or to shorten the activity to fit into a tight schedule. Ways **to expand** the unit are also provided to challenge advanced students and to continue a lesson that needs further development in the classroom.

A **teacher script** is provided to make framing the activity simple and fun. It is designed to be an aid in addressing the beginning learners. You may choose to use it as is or to modify it to fit your own teaching style.

The lesson plan for each activity unit ends with suggestions for **evaluation and processing.**

Overview

Cooperative Learning Activities for Language Arts begins the path of language arts discovery. The book is geared for children who are just beginning to show readiness for cooperative work. The exercises are set in a travel-related context that is familiar and easy to understand. Students begin by examining the forms of travel with which they are most familiar— travel on land by cars, bicycles, trains, buses, and trucks. They follow up with concepts of travel by sea and by air, learning the fundamentals of language arts while becoming more comfortable with their peers and more knowledgeable about the world around them.

Beginning the Book

To begin cooperative learning on a successful note, focus on the whole-class activities on pages 5-8. In this way, students can begin to interact as a whole-class and then in pairs in a non-threatening and positive manner.

These activities will help you build an attitude of friendliness and cooperation in your classroom before attempting to organize student groups. Additionally, whole-class and pair activities will provide you with opportunities for assessing individuals to best determine the members for each group. (See "Setting Up Groups," pages 9-14.)

Cooperative Learning Groups

This book has been written for a classroom with thirty students, or six groups of five. Simply add or subtract groups, or students in a group, to best serve your class's particular needs. Remember, in cooperative learning, it is best to use an uneven number of students in each group whenever possible.

What About Results?

One of the best reasons for introducing cooperative learning activities throughout the curriculum is that children benefit from them in distinctly observable ways. After completing the activities in this book, look for student improvement and mastery in the following areas:

- ❖ Oral presentation
- ❖ The writing process
- ❖ Cognitive and high-order learning skills
- ❖ Communication and conflict-resolution skills
- ❖ Self-esteem
- ❖ Ability to work with classmates
- ❖ Understanding of travel and transportation

How Else Can This Book Be Used?

Besides its usefulness with the beginning learner, this book has many possibilities for use with ESL students. As the concepts are of a beginning nature, children with English as a second language will be helped by the simplified themes of each activity.

Whole-Classroom Readiness and Activities

Easing into Cooperative Learning

Prepare your students for cooperative learning by conducting whole-class cooperative activities. Whole-class activities are especially conducive to creating a comfortable, safe environment in which students have some knowledge and understanding of one another. It is helpful to ease into the cooperative experience since many beginning students have never had the experience of cooperative interaction.

Parallel Players and Pre-Cooperative Learners

The younger the children are, the less comfortable they will feel in group situations. Most toddlers and preschoolers parallel play. This means that they play near each other at separate tasks. To begin the transition from parallel play to pre-cooperative learning, teachers can focus on teaching children how to get along within the classroom setting. Page 6 offers many activities that support this.

Concepts such as sharing and taking turns are understood by the pre-cooperative learner, and while a pre-cooperative learner may not always feel comfortable trying to share or take turns, these ideas are ones he or she will recognize. Remember, becoming a cooperative learner is a process. Many adults have yet to master the idea in their work situations. Be aware of your students. When they have had enough of a cooperative activity, turn to a less stressful and more autonomous one.

Partner Play

Cooperation is an important component in any classroom. When children cooperate, they have the opportunity to think about and assimilate new ideas.

Use the whole-class activities on page 8 to nurture the cooperative atmosphere within your classroom. Each activity is followed by a suggested partner play. To help ease your children into the concept of cooperative learning, allow them this time to work with one partner only.

You may wish to have your students become very comfortable with partner play before beginning the cooperative activities in the rest of the book, or you may find it beneficial to use both group and partner activities, depending on your students' learning needs.

Whole-Classroom Readiness and Activities (cont.)

1. **Shoe Hunt/Partner Hunt:** Students can use the pattern on page 7 to color two matching shoes. They will write their names on the provided lines. Half the students can then put one "shoe" into a box, bowl, or other container, and leave the second shoe on their desks. The other half will take turns picking a shoe and matching it to the one on the owner's desk. The student whose shoe was picked will then become that student's partner. Each set of partners will talk together to find out three things about one another. They can write the things on the shoes. Use the completed shoes for a bulletin board display.

   This activity is a good ice breaker for shy children or those who do not know each other. Used at the beginning of the school year, it will set the stage for building cooperative teams based on friendly interaction.

2. **Secret Secret:** Choose a leader to begin. Have students stand in a circle. The first person tells the second person a secret. It is then repeated until it reaches the end of the circle and is said aloud. Have the person who began the secret and the person who heard it last compare the differences in the secret. This activity will help students to understand the importance of listening carefully in their cooperative groups.

3. **Walking Through the Neighborhood, I Saw a . . . :**
   This is a whole-class participation alphabet game. Students stand or sit in a circle. Choose someone to lead with the sentence-starter, "I was walking through the neighborhood, and I saw a . . . ." He or she fills in the blank with something that starts with an "A." The next person in the group must think of something that begins with the letter "B," and so on with the rest of the alphabet. (If there are more students after "Z," return to the beginning of the alphabet.)

   You may wish to begin the activity by holding a whole-class discussion about the possible things that a child might see during a walk through the neighborhood. You may also alter the first sentence as desired. For example, you may begin, "In my house I saw a . . . ," or "I went to the city and saw a . . . ."

4. **Alphabet Name Game:** Give each student a soup bowl with alphabet macaroni or paper letters. Write a word on the board. The first student to spell the word with his/her alphabet letters is the winner of the round. Next, have students work in pairs to spell as many words as they can with their letters, making a written list of the words they spell. Beginning readers can spell their names by locating the appropriate alphabet letters. This activity increases letter recognition and spelling skills while at the same time introducing friendly competition. (You can also play non-competitively.)

5. **Learn To Take Turns:** Explore the many ways of taking turns. For example, vote, flip coins, let a neutral party decide, draw straws, draw names, guess a number or a letter, or simply take turns being leader.

Whole-Classroom Readiness and Activities (cont.)

See page 6, "Shoe Hunt/Partner Hunt," for directions.

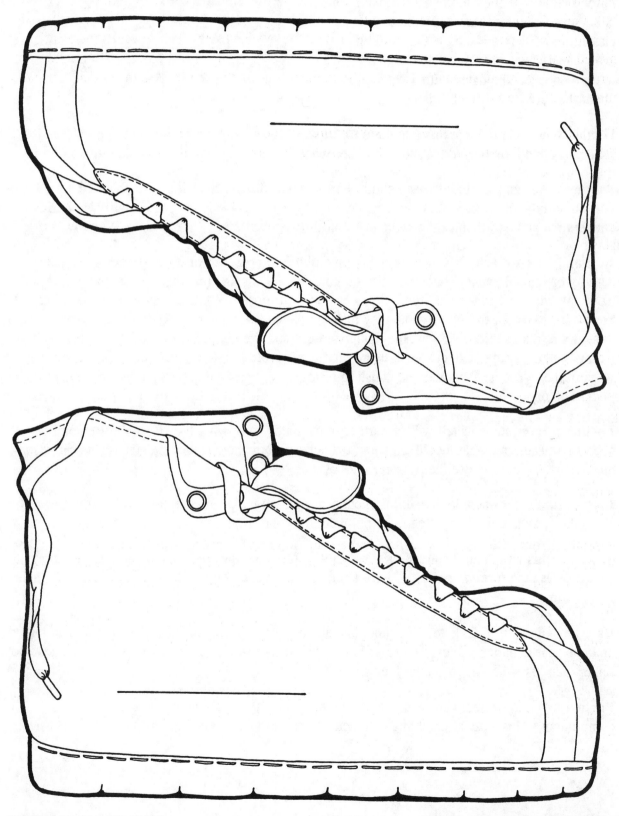

Whole-Classroom Readiness and Activities (cont.)

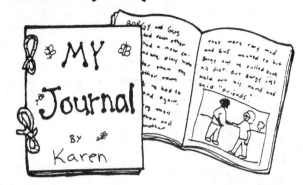

1. **Picture Journal:** This activity can be used for individual and partner interaction. Have each child start a picture journal. When any classroom activity ends, have the children draw and write about the activity. Each journal entry can be dated with a notation about the activity to which it is referring.

   Let the students know that this journal is for them. There is no one right way to do it. It is just for fun. They can look back on it and remember what they did in class and how they felt about it.

   Partners: Assign a partner to each child. Partners will discuss their journal entries. This activity will not only help children relax in a cooperative learning environment, but it will also build cooperative and communicative skills in a non-threatening way.

2. **Rest and Remember:** This activity will help children prepare for or unwind after a classroom activity or special event. Have the children go to their seats and rest their heads on their desks. You may wish to dim the classroom lights or play soft music. While the students are resting, ask them to think about the activity that they just completed. Ask them to picture the activity, see it as a mental movie, and decide what they liked and did not like about it. Ask them how they felt— happy, sad, angry, excited, etc. Ask them what they would like to do differently next time they work in their groups. You may then wish to follow up by reading the students a short, happy poem or story.

   Partners: Have students talk with a partner immediately following the "Rest and Remember" exercise, discussing what they liked about the activity they have just completed. This can also be another opportunity to use their picture journals.

3. **Letter Home:** This activity is helpful in encouraging language and memory skills. It also engenders parental and parent/child participation in your program.

   Have students write and illustrate, or simply illustrate, what they did in a cooperative learning activity. Use the form on page 9 or have students create their own. Students can then take their letters home.

   Have students return the letters to school and share what their parents thought about the activity and their participation. These letters will also help you to stay in contact with parents consistently, rather than just when there is a problem.

   Partners: Have partners view each other's letter home and make one positive comment or compliment. This activity encourages students to support each other, and it promotes self esteem.

Parent Letter

Dear _____,

Here is a picture of what my cooperative family group did today.

I helped my group by:

_____

_____

_____

My favorite part was:

_____

_____

_____

Love,

_____

- -

Parent Comments:

_____

_____

_____

Note from the Teacher: Thank you for supporting your child in his/her cooperative learning experience. I welcome all parent volunteers. Please write your number here if you would like a phone call.

Thank you,

_____

Name: _____

Name of Child: _____

Phone: _____

Selecting Cooperative Groups

Picture This

It is day one of a new school year. Mrs. Sumersover walks shakily into her classroom and gazes out at the sea of expectant, childish faces. She feels stressed. She would like to add cooperative learning to her program this year, but she is not really sure how to do it. Most of her experience has been in traditional classroom settings. She spent the summer at the beach reading information on cooperative learning, but she still feels unsure and uncomfortable. She does not have tenure, the economy is in recession, and she can not afford to make any mistakes. At the same time, other teachers have already successfully incorporated cooperative learning into their classrooms. Mrs. Sumersover needs assistance from a friendly, clear, non-threatening source.

I Need a Vacation!

Most of us are not this worried about how to incorporate current teaching trends into our classroom, but many of us have shared Mrs. Sumersover's sense of dread. Mrs. Sumersover needs a clear, concise, stress-free, and fun resource to help her pull her classroom and her curriculum together.

Icing on the Cake

Mrs. Beterthanu walks to her classroom on the first day of school. Eyes follow her. How does anyone who teaches manage to look that put together? She opens the door to her classroom with satisfaction. A giant fabric palm tree rises from the center of the room. Gleaming computers shine in a neat row against the wall, keyboards smiling, anticipating little fingers. In one corner, a wooden reading area built to look like a real tree house stands like a monument to learning. How nice to have a handy husband!

Top of the Class

She just needs one more thing: a cooperative learning plan as well prepared and nifty as her adorable classroom. She needs cutting-edge materials to make her curriculum sparkle as much as her room. She is a professional and a perfectionist, and she has to have the best.

Making It Happen

Maybe you know both of these teachers. Both of them could benefit by streamlined, easy, effective ways of incorporating cooperative learning into their classrooms successfully—the first time. The following chapter gives you quick and easy guidelines on how to set up your cooperative learning classroom. Blackline master forms have been included whenever possible to streamline the process.

Selecting Cooperative Groups (cont.)

Kinds of Learners

While all children are different, and certainly children's abilities and skill levels can change, most students fit into one of these four categories of learners:

❖ High Achievers

❖ Special Needs Students

❖ English as a Second Language (ESL) Students

❖ Competent Achievers

When selecting the members of cooperative groups, be sure to create a mix of all four areas. To help determine the members of each of your cooperative groups, the following descriptions offer some easily recognizable qualities that learners of the same "type" share.

High Achievers

High achievers can fall into two categories. Current educational thought holds that while some students are considered high achievers based on their I.Q., others are labeled this way not so much because of exceptional intelligence but because of exceptional motivation. When looking for the high achievers, consider these qualities:

❖ High I.Q.

❖ Good verbal skills

❖ Good oral communication skills

❖ Problem-solving ability

❖ Good study and concentration skills

❖ Academic excellence

❖ Interest in learning

❖ Leadership skills

❖ Exceptional talent

❖ Multifaceted interests and abilities

While there are certainly other ways to determine high achievers, and not all high achievers share the same qualities, this partial list will help you know what qualities to consider. High achievers can bring ideas, leadership, and assistance into a cooperative group.

Special Needs Students

While special needs students can be high achievers, low achievers, ESL, or English speaking, the commonality is that they all need special assistance. Some may have difficult family situations, like a divorce or separation, while others may be diagnosed with severe emotional or behavioral problems. While the special needs student requires extra care, placing him/her in the right situation just might diminish or solve his/her problem. A sad, distracted child might be placed in a group with a fun, happy child, thus giving that child a model for growth. Children, like adults, benefit by the positive attitudes of those around them. Look for these qualities when determining your special needs students:

❖ History of emotional or behavioral problems

❖ Anger

❖ Low level of socialization skills

❖ Recovery from a recent illness

❖ A.D.D. student

❖ Recent family upset

❖ Low motivation

❖ Quick frustration

❖ New to the country, state, city, or school

While there are other things that may contribute to a child's place in the special needs category, these qualities will give you a guiding framework. Remember that this group, more than any of the others, is transitory. It is very possible during the length of a school year for a child's situation to change enough to either remove him/her or add him/her to this category.

Selecting Cooperative Groups (cont.)

English as a Second Language (ESL) Students

ESL students are usually challenged by the circumstances of their learning. Most of us have no idea how traumatic it is to be relocated to a new country, with little or no knowledge of the language, the customs, the culture, or the people. Moreover, often these students are without friends, having left their old ones behind.

ESL students come in every variety under the sun. Some are extremely well educated in their own language, learn English quickly, and assimilate with relative ease. Others have frightening, painful experiences when it comes to success in their new schools.

ESL students have a special place in this book, one that will help you to help them bring their own cultures into the learning experience. Rather than be ostracized for their differences, ESL students will be able to assume the role of "cultural diplomat." It is the intention of this book to support multicultural awareness and education wherever possible. By its very content, *Cooperative Learning Activities for Language Arts* will make the challenge of working successfully with ESL students a little easier.

When looking for students to classify as ESL, be aware of the following qualities:
- ❖ Recently arrived from another country
- ❖ American-born, but in a home where a language other than English is predominant
- ❖ Speaks English well, but has not mastered reading or writing in English
- ❖ English-speaking, but under the care of one for whom English is a second language
- ❖ Stuck in the "silent interval" of language acquisition

Once provided with the special attention they need, ESL students often turn out to be competent or high achievers. The cooperative learning activities in this book will help you to access the strengths of these students and to provide them with many self-esteem building opportunities.

Competent Achievers

Unfortunately, competent achievers, often those who "do not give any trouble," just as often get very little teacher attention. In a classroom with 30 or more children, it is the competent child who is "all right" and gets left to fend for him/herself. When singling out competent achievers in your classroom, remember that these children should be rewarded and not penalized for being less demanding. Those with behavior problems should not see their negativity reinforced by the focus always remaining on them. Furthermore, in every group of competent achievers, there are a number of hidden high achievers who will blossom with the proper self-esteem-building attention and experiences.

When looking for competent achievers, watch for the following signs:
- ❖ Students whom you do not often think about
- ❖ Average grades
- ❖ Oral and written language skills around grade level
- ❖ Shyness or quietness
- ❖ Pleasant low-key personalities
- ❖ Low resistance to the learning experience
- ❖ A marked willingness to follow

While not all competent achievers fit this mold, it is at least safe to say that these are the children you are likely to think less about than any of the others. They are the children who stand in line, raise their hands, and rarely cause any disturbances. Competent achievers are the people who keep the world running smoothly, in and out of the classroom, and for this they deserve much praise and a loving hug.

Selecting Cooperative Groups (cont.)

Now What?

Now that you know what to look for in determining the different "learning types" in your classroom, use the blackline master on page 14 to simplify the process.

It may be fun to give each cooperative group a travel-related name. For example, the groups might be named after continents, oceans, countries, or modes of transportation.

As far as group size is concerned, five is a good number. Therefore, if you have thirty students, you will create six groups, each consisting of five individuals. In cooperative learning situations, an uneven number is an asset during the decision process. (No "hung jury," so to speak!) When selecting the members of each group, here is what to remember:

The "Salad Bowl"

Rather than as a melting pot, a situation in which everyone's individual traits melt together, the ideal cooperative learning situation should be thought of as a salad bowl. In a salad bowl, all ingredients (individual learning types) mix together. They create synergy while remaining individuals. For purposes of explanation and ease, follow this simple recipe:

Cooperative Learning Salad Bowl

Combine the following ingredients:

❖ High achievers

❖ Special needs students

❖ ESL students

❖ Competent achievers

Select five according to taste. Flavor with the following random differences:

❖ Genders

❖ Personality types

❖ Ethnicities

❖ Learning styles

Introduce each ingredient into the mix slowly, stirring in large pieces of humor, understanding, cooperation, and support. Let the mix remain together—qualities, strengths, and weaknesses intermingling. Facilitate ingredients rising to the occasion . . . and ENJOY THE RESULTS!

Selecting Cooperative Groups (cont.)

Legend

HA: High Achiever
SN: Special Needs Student
ESL: English as a Second Language Student
CA: Competent Achiever

Group One (example)	Group Two	Group Three
(HA)	( )	( )
(CA)	( )	( )
(CA)	( )	( )
(SN)	( )	( )
(ESL)	( )	( )
Notes:_____	Notes:_____	Notes:_____
_____	_____	_____
_____	_____	_____

Group Four	Group Five	Group Six
( )	( )	( )
( )	( )	( )
( )	( )	( )
( )	( )	( )
( )	( )	( )
Notes:_____	Notes:_____	Notes:_____
_____	_____	_____
_____	_____	_____

Parent Introduction Letter

Dear Parents,

In our classroom this year, we will be approaching language arts in a very interesting way. We will be studying the various forms of land, sea, and air travel. While doing so, every student will have a chance to work cooperatively in pairs or in groups. This will give everyone a chance to take part in many enriching learning experiences.

Here is where you come in. Cooperative learning is a special kind of learning. Rather than sitting in a chair all day and learning solely by rote, your child will be working in small groups. He/she will have the chance to get more personalized attention while learning how to interact effectively with peers. Also, as our subject for this unit is language arts, there will be a real emphasis on the mechanics of writing clear sentences and paragraphs, ending with a published whole-class effort.

Because of this different way of learning, parent volunteers are very important. If you have several hours a week that you would like to spend in your child's classroom, it will be a wonderful help to the class and it will prove a very fond memory for your child.

I realize, of course, that most of you have extremely busy schedules and that some of you will not be able to take part in our classroom. However, there are many ways to take part in your child's learning experience, and I would be happy to speak with you about how you can get involved. Thank you for your support!

Sincerely,

_____

If you would like me to call you, please fill in the information below and send it to me.

Name: _____

Child's Name: _____

Phone: _____

Assessment and Portfolios

Make It Manageable

Assessing your students' progress does not have to be a formidable task. Included for you here are two handy forms to lighten the load and consolidate your efforts. First, there is the "Individual Anecdotal Record" on page 17. Use this to keep a daily record of individual student progress in each activity or area. Make sure to date these records and to include them in a student portfolio. For more information and other forms, refer to Teacher Created Material's *Portfolios and Other Assessments*.

Next, you will find "Reflections on the Activity" on page 18. This form is for students to fill out after each activity. Again, store them in their portfolios. This form will help you gauge how the students are doing and how they are feeling about the activities.

A Word About Portfolios

Create portfolios out of small boxes or shirt gift boxes, something that can stack but at the same time is big enough for bulky projects. It is important when assessing your students by the portfolio method to make parents aware that they will not receive as much take-home work. It is always a good idea to make parents aware of your assessment process and make them part of it at the very beginning of the year. Inform them every step of the way and you will save yourself some big headaches. You may even get some interested and wonderful parent helpers!

Assessment and the Pre-Cooperative Learner

Finally, remember that cooperative learning is a difficult concept. Preschoolers and some primary children prefer, and are far better at, parallel play. The transition is usually a slow one. Keep in mind that it is a process, and adjust your expectations accordingly.

Have Fun!

This book has been designed with the idea that not only will your students like the activities and have a good time, but so will you. Choose activities that you really love. Do not feel you have to do them all or that you must do them word-for-word. Together with your own creativity, the activities in this book will equal a fabulous year. Good luck!

Record Forms

Run off a stack of these forms and keep them—one for each student in your class—in a three-ring binder. Make your notes right on the appropriate form. When a page is filled up, it can be replaced with a new page and the filled page placed in the student's portfolio. No time is lost transcribing information!

- -

Individual Anecdotal Record

Name _____

Date	Comment

Record Forms (cont.)

Run off copies of this form for your students to use as they start the process of reflecting on their own achievements. This particular form was designed for primary children and requires little writing. Allow plenty of time for the children to look over and think about their work. When the form has been completed, attach it to the work (if possible) and include it in each student's portfolio.

- -

Reflections on the Activity

Name_____ Date _____

When I look back on the work I have done, I feel . . .

I have gotten better in . . .

_____

_____

_____

_____

I am really proud of . . .

_____

_____

Next time I do an activity like this, I will . . .

_____

_____

Language Arts Activity Centers

Centers for Language Arts

The cooperative activities in this book focus on land, sea, and air. In support of them, three exciting and easy-to-make center ideas are suggested on pages 20-23. They will pull your room together in a decorative and functional way, and they will definitely catch the interest of your students! The directions and ideas that follow will help you set up imaginative centers that will make learning fun and your classroom a showplace.

Car Center: an automobile for overland adventure!

Boat Center: a motor boat for high-speed learning!

Plane Center: an airplane fueled with fun!

All Three!

While some teachers may wish to have only one center at a time set up in their rooms, it is possible to set up all three if space permits. Each center requires a *little* artistic talent, some readily available supplies, and an afternoon or two. Teachers with advanced students may wish to make the center development part of a class project.

Dashboards and Instruments

Dashboard and instrument blackline masters have been provided to make each vehicle center as realistic as possible. Simply copy the patterns from pages 24-29 on an enlarged setting to make the dashboard/instrument area of your center as large as possible. If photocopy enlargement is not available, project the image from an overhead projector onto some butcher paper, trace, and cut out.

Make It Yourself

To create your centers you will need the following materials:

- ❖ one large refrigerator box per center
- ❖ poster paint
- ❖ several small student chairs
- ❖ glue
- ❖ tape
- ❖ dowels
- ❖ scissors
- ❖ cardboard
- ❖ paintbrushes
- ❖ construction paper
- ❖ ruler or yardstick
- ❖ directions on pages 20-23
- ❖ dashboard/instrument patterns on pages 24-29

Car and Motor Boat

Follow these directions to make the car center. See page 21 for the necessary variations to make a motor boat.

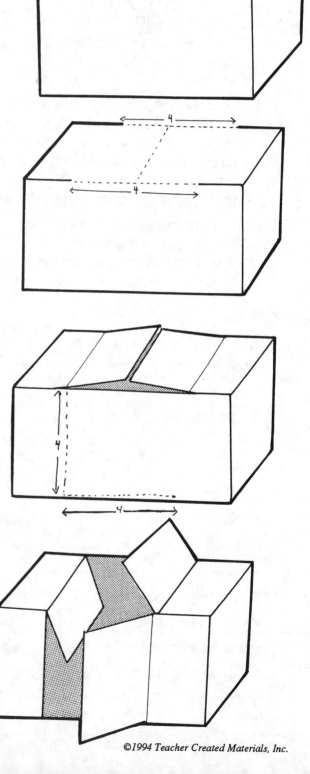

1. Close and seal a large refrigerator box.

2. Cut across the top center and about 4 feet (1.2 meters) across on either edge.

3. On one side, cut straight down from the end of the cut you made along the edge (step 2). Then, cut 4 feet (1.2 meters) across the bottom. This will make a door. (Do not cut two doors, because the box cannot stand without the support.)

4. On the top, fold up the right flap to make a windshield. Fold down the left flap to enclose the "trunk."

Car and Motor Boat (cont.)

5. Add black construction paper wheels with gray paper "hubcaps."

6. Add headlights made of silver paper. For a fancier touch, cut the tops from two plastic 1-liter bottles. Inside each bottle bottom, secure a flashlight so that the lit end is facing through the plastic. Secure one to each side of the front of the car. Turn the lights on for night driving!

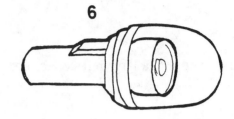

6

7. Enlarge, color, and cut out the car dashboard (pages 24-25). Attach.

8. Cut a steering wheel from cardboard. Attach.

9. Paint. Add interesting touches, like bumper stickers and personalized license plates.

10. Add chairs inside for the seats.

11. This is what the completed car should look like.

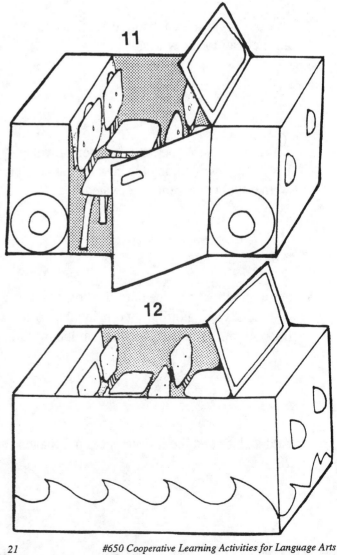

11

12

12. Motor Boat Variation: Follow the steps to make a car, except you will need to make a larger seating area, you should not cut out a door, and you will need the boat instrument patterns on pages 26-27.

Airplane

Follow these directions to make the airplane center.

1

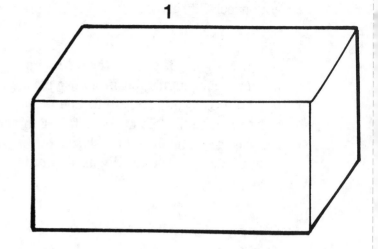

1. Close and seal a large refrigerator box.

2. Cut wings out from the sides, leaving the top of the wings attached.

2-3

3. Cut out cockpit area, being careful not to cut all the way to the wings.

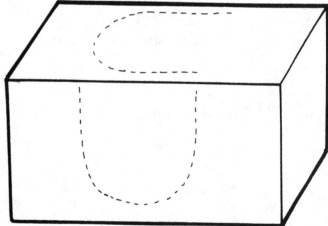

4. Lift the wings. Tape long, wooden dowels under each wing along the edge of the cockpit so that the wings remain elevated.

5. Paint an airplane shape onto the box. You can add clouds and a bird or two painted across the bottom. You can also add a cardboard tail.

4-6

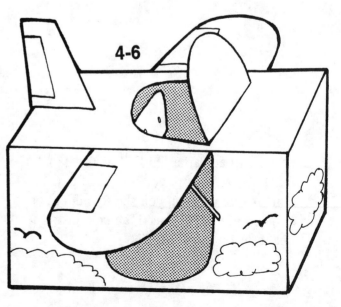

6. Add a chair and the instrument panel (pages 28-29).

Rowboat Variation

Follow these directions to make a rowboat center.

1. Close and seal a large refrigerator box.

2. Slice a large oblong out of the top of the box.

3. From the oblong, cut two oars.

4. Paint the oars and boat. You can add water painted across the bottom. Add chairs.

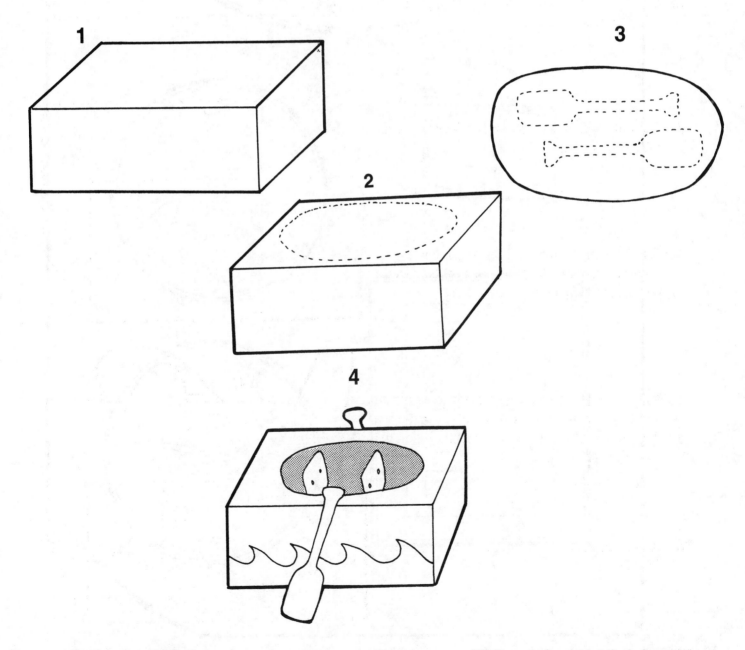

Car Dash

24

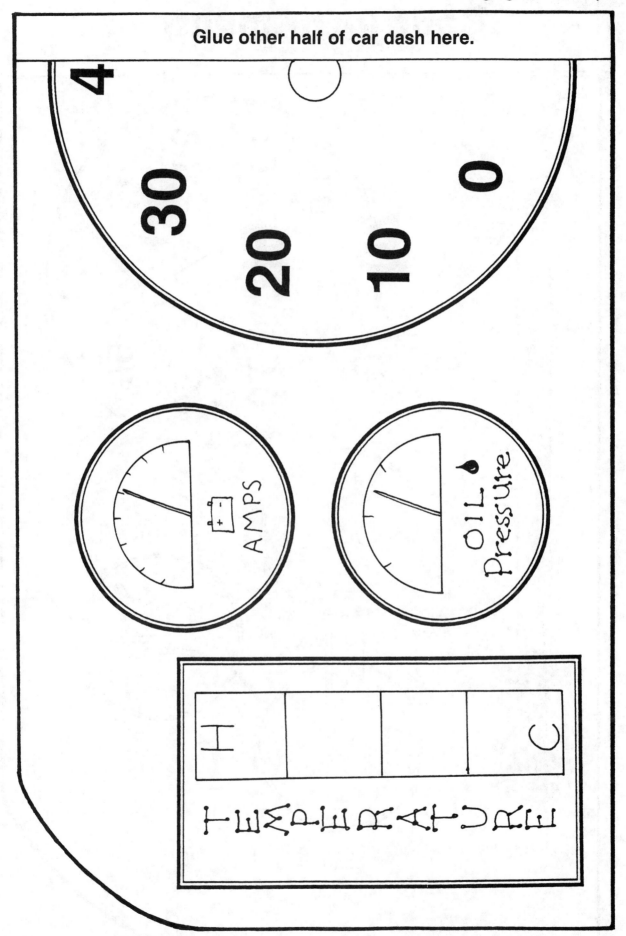

Glue other half of car dash here.

4

30

0

20

10

AMPS

OIL Pressure

H

C

TEMPERATURE

Boat Instruments

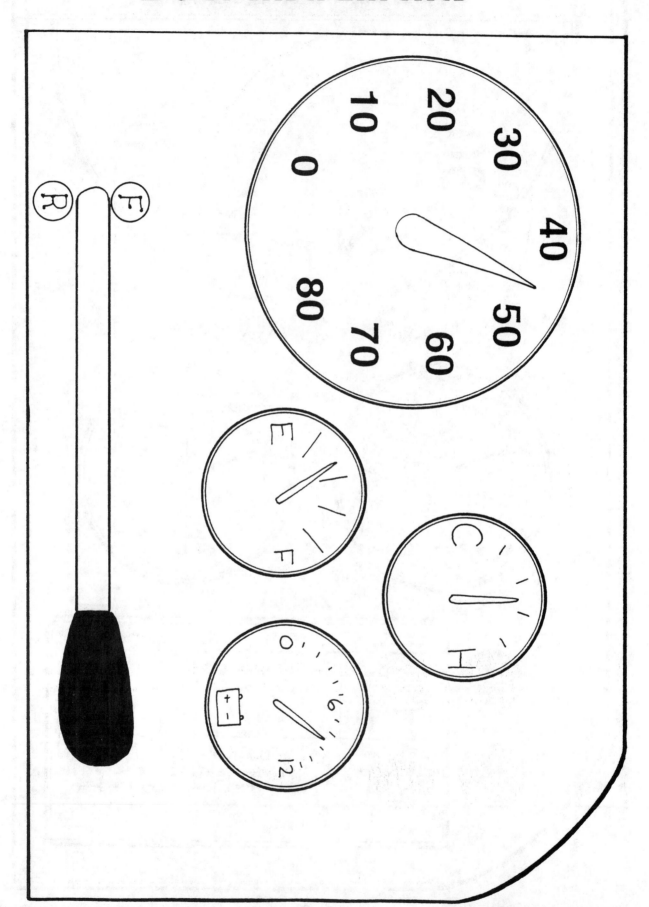

Glue other half of boat instruments here.

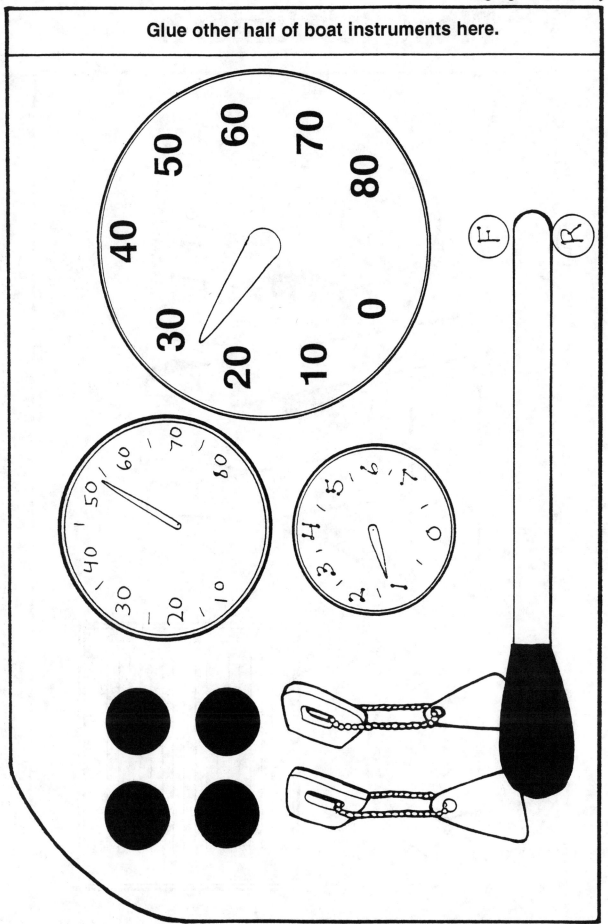

Plane Instruments

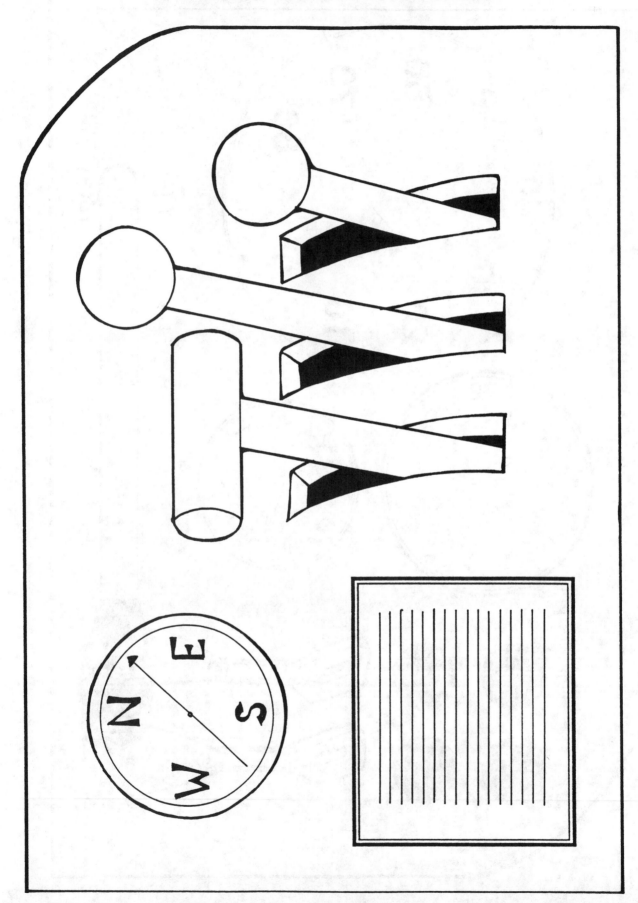

Glue other half of plane instruments here.

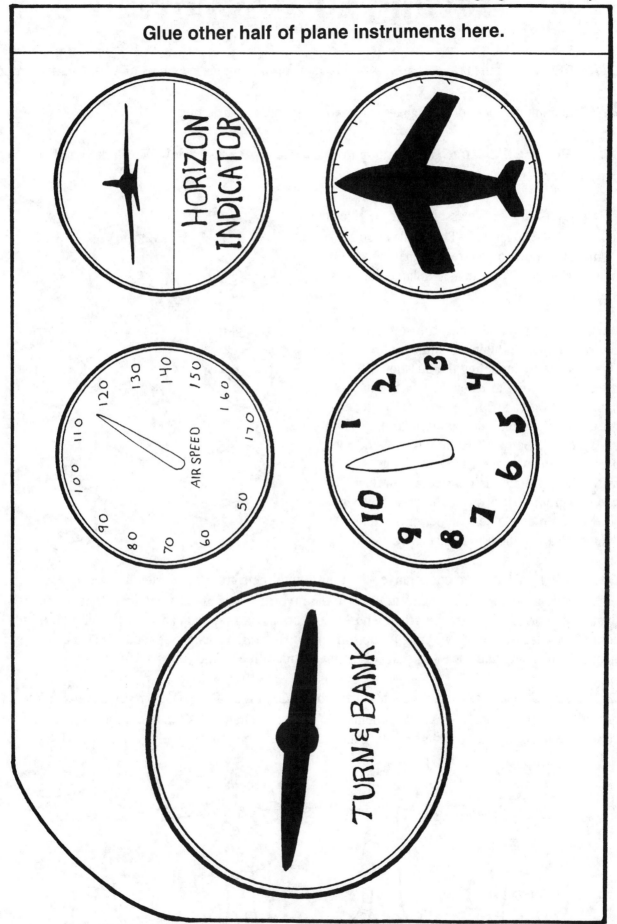

Getting to Know Me

Purpose: To establish rapport and a sense of comfort among the members of a cooperative group.

Skills: communication, oral language, decision making, and listening

Materials Per Student: "Getting to Know Me" (page 32), "How We Work Together" (page 33), pencils or pens, and coloring materials

Procedures: As a class, go over the rules on "How We Work Together." These rules will let students know how to be effective members of a cooperative team. You can also enlarge the rules to poster size to display in the classroom.

Next, tell the children that they are going to get to know each other. Explain the simple information they will share by modeling the questions and answers on "Getting to Know Me." (See the teacher script on page 31.) Now, ask the students to sit in a circle in their cooperative groups. Give each student a "Getting To Know Me" worksheet. Students will answer the questions about themselves and share their answers with their individual groups. If possible, have each group work with an older student helper or a parent volunteer to assist them in this activity.

To Simplify: Have pre-cooperative learners sit with their groups and each think of his/her favorite food. Then, ask the students to listen to the favorite foods of each person in their group. Explain that a prize will go to the group whose members listen best and can tell what their "family's" favorite foods are. Offer the winning group something small like stickers or candy. (This activity will enhance the listening and speaking skills of the pre-cooperative learner.)

To Expand: Have advanced students share their "Getting to Know Me" pages and discuss their similarities and differences. Next, have them color their pages and make them into a book. Students may work together on a cover, thus creating their group's cover cooperatively.

Getting to Know Me (cont.)

Teacher Script:

Today we are going to begin working in our family groups. We are going to get to know each other and find out a little bit about each other. Before we start, let's go over our "How We Work Together" rules. *(Read the rules aloud.)* Let's talk about what these rules mean. *(At this point, let the children discuss the rules and give examples of what they mean.)* Good, now I think we are almost ready to start.

I need someone to play the "Getting to Know Me" game with me to show the class how. Okay, Amber will help me. Everyone, please look at your paper. There are five statements. The first one says, "My favorite color is _____." I will tell Amber my favorite color and then I will let her tell me her favorite color. We will both take turns talking and listening to each other, and we will try to remember each other's favorite color. When we work in our groups, everyone will get a turn to tell the rest of the group about his or her favorite color, and so forth. *(Model the activity.)*

Now let's all sit in our family groups and give it a try. Your helper will help you get started and answer your questions. I will walk around the room and help you, too.

Evaluation and Processing: Evaluate this exercise by spending time with each group during the activity to see how they are doing. You will be able to gauge their success easily by interacting with each group. Process with your whole class by giving students a chance to share their group's answers and tell what they like the most about the activity.

Name _____

Getting to Know Me

Complete these statements. When everyone is finished, tell your family group your answers and listen to theirs.

1. My favorite color is _____.

2. My favorite food is _____.

3. I have _____ brothers and _____ sisters.

4. My favorite toy is _____.

5. My favorite animal is _____.

Use this space to draw a picture about some of your statements.

How We Work Together

1. When we work in groups, we always take turns.

2. We listen when other people talk.

3. Everyone in the group gets to have a turn.

4. If we cannot agree on something, we vote.

5. If we have a problem, we try to work it out. We do not fight.

6. If we do not know what to do or we have a question, we ask the group first and then the teacher.

Setting the Scene: Land Mural

Purpose: To introduce or enhance whole-class and cooperative group skills while building a reading/writing vocabulary associated with land travel.

Skills: word identification, reading comprehension, writing of upper and lower case letters, oral communication (both speaking and listening), decision making, and art

Materials for the Class: large sheets of butcher paper mounted on the classroom wall (see procedures given below and the sample on page 36), drawing paper, pre-cut strips for labels, old magazines, pencils, markers and other coloring materials, scissors, staplers, and copies of land travel pictures (pages 38-44)

Procedures: In advance, draw and color on the butcher paper a mural background depicting land, sea, and air. These areas should be obvious, but the degree of detail will depend on the grade level you are teaching. You can use white butcher paper and paint it or try three wide strips of colored paper (brown or green on the bottom for land, dark blue in the middle for sea, and light blue on the top for air). The size and shape of this mural will depend on the size of your classroom and the wall space you can devote to it.

When the class is together, review the group rules on page 33. Then, begin the mural activity with a whole-class discussion in which students think of and name various kinds of land transportation. Write what they say on the board. Make sure that all the things suggested on pages 38-44 are included.

When students are ready to go to their cooperative groups, assign one or more types of transportation to each group. The students will work together to draw, color, and cut out examples of their type(s) of transportation, mounting them on the land section of the mural. (You can use the patterns provided, or students can draw their own.) They will also label each mode of transportation, using the words you wrote on the board to verify spelling. If possible, have each group work with an older student or parent volunteer.

To Simplify: For pre-cooperative learners, provide the pictures on pages 38-44 and prewritten labels. Have students work in their groups to match the pictures and labels. When all agree that the pictures and labels are correctly matched, students may mount them on the mural. Older students and parent volunteers will be very helpful here.

Setting the Scene: Land Mural (cont.)

To Expand: After advanced students have finished their pictures and labels and mounted them on the mural, have them begin to make travel dictionaries. These dictionaries can be kept in notebooks or on sheets of paper fastened with brads or yarn. For the cover, students may wish to use page 37.

Each page of the dictionary should have a letter of the alphabet at the top. Students will write travel words on the appropriate pages and then use them as a spelling help for their writing activities. Students who wish to may add definitions and illustrations. These dictionaries will be ongoing through the year and can be stored in the students' portfolios. They can be displayed at Open House or during a culminating activity or party.

Teacher Script:

Today we are going to talk about traveling by land. We will meet first as a large group and then move into our cooperative learning groups. Before we start, let's go over our "How We Work Together Rules." Everyone, please look at this poster. Let's review what these rules mean. *(At this point, the teacher should let the children discuss the rules and give examples of what they mean.)* Good. Now I think we're ready to start.

Look at the bulletin board. This is the start of a mural that you are going to complete. The bottom part will show ways that we can travel on land. The middle part will show ways to travel on water, and the top part will show ways to travel in the air. We'll take care of the sea and air later. Right now we'll just talk about land travel.

Raise your hand as soon as you can think of a way to travel on land. *(The teacher accepts all suggestions and prints the words on the chalkboard.)* If that list names every kind of land travel you can think of, we are ready for the next part of the activity.

Each small group will have a kind of land travel for its own. Some of you may need to do more than one kind. *(Teacher makes assignments.)* You can color the pictures that I will give you, cut pictures out of magazines, or draw your own. Talk to the other members of your group to plan what you are doing. For example, group 2 is responsible for trains. They will want to decide who will make the engine and who will make other kinds of cars.

When your pictures are finished, you will take a strip of paper and write the name of your picture on it. *(Model.)* Then you will put your picture and its name in a good place on the mural. The parent or student aide in your group can help you if you need it. I will walk around the room to help and answer questions.

Evaluation and Processing: Evaluate this activity by spending time with each group, listening to their discussion, and watching their creation of a product. (Keep at hand copies of the "Individual Anecdotal Record" on page 17, and make notes to put in each student's portfolio.) Process with the whole class by looking at and admiring the mural. Have students tell what they liked best about the activity and what they would still like to do. Allow interested, motivated students to add to the mural as an extra-credit homework assignment.

Sample Mural

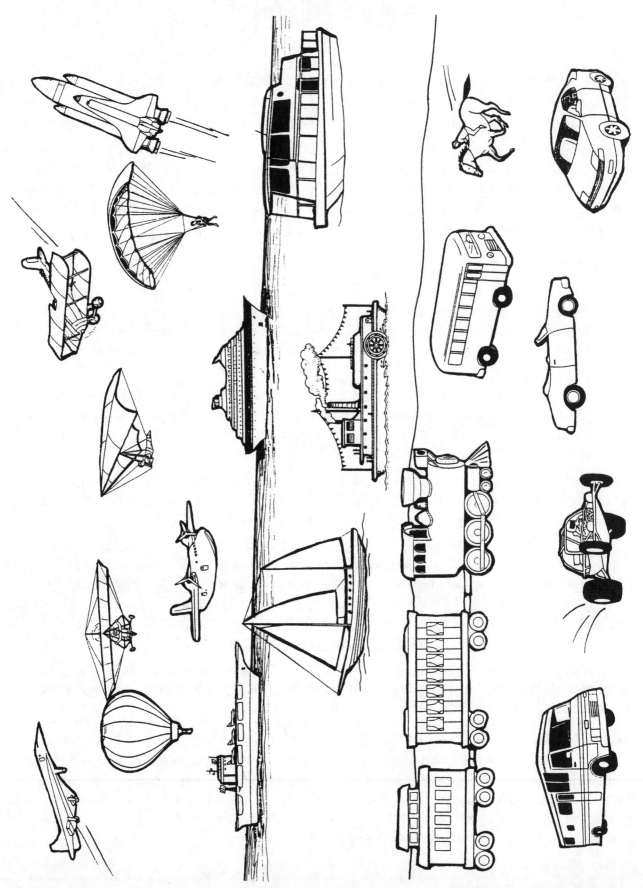

Travel
Dictionary

Land Travel Pictures

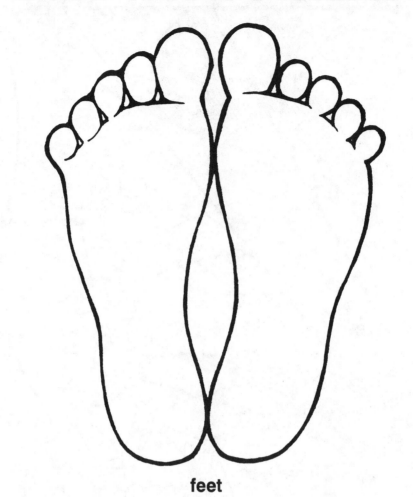

feet

horseback

Land Travel Pictures (cont.)

car *(coupe)*

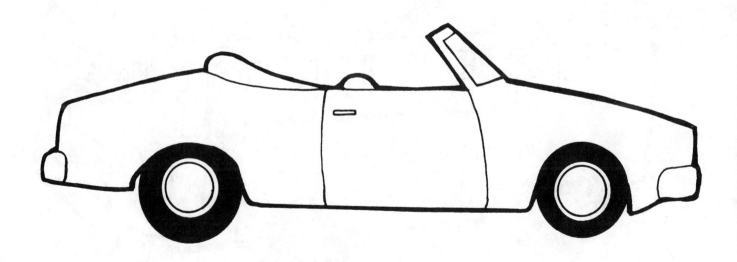

car *(convertible)*

Land Travel Pictures (cont.)

dune buggy

bus

Land Travel Pictures (cont.)

train engine

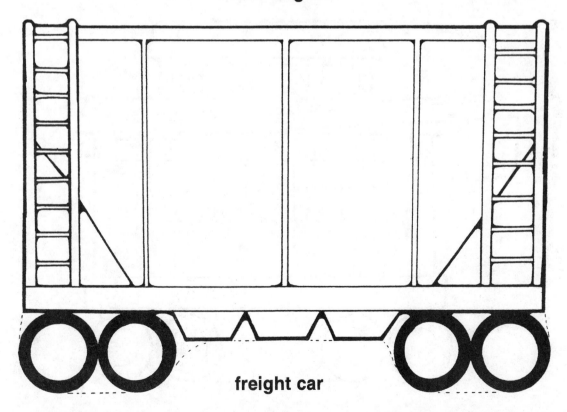

freight car

Land Travel Pictures (cont.)

passenger car

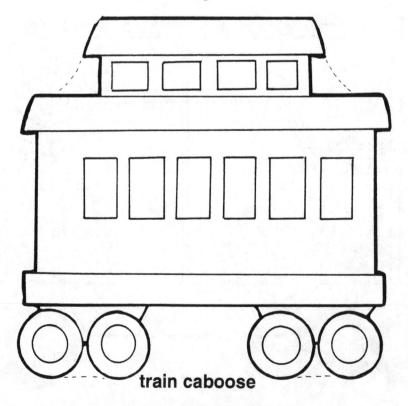

train caboose

Land Travel Pictures (cont.)

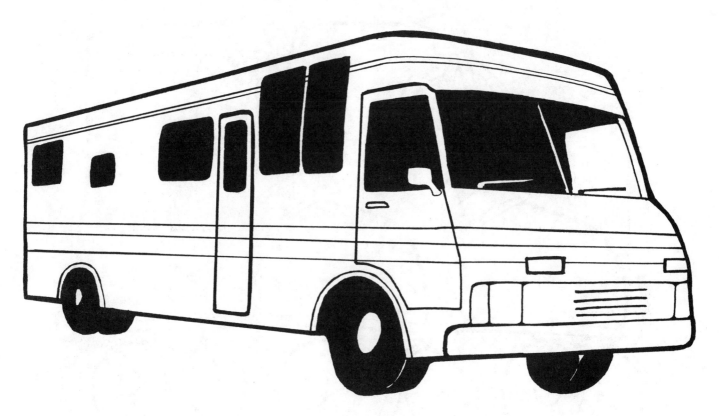

motor home

bicycle

Land Travel Pictures (cont.)

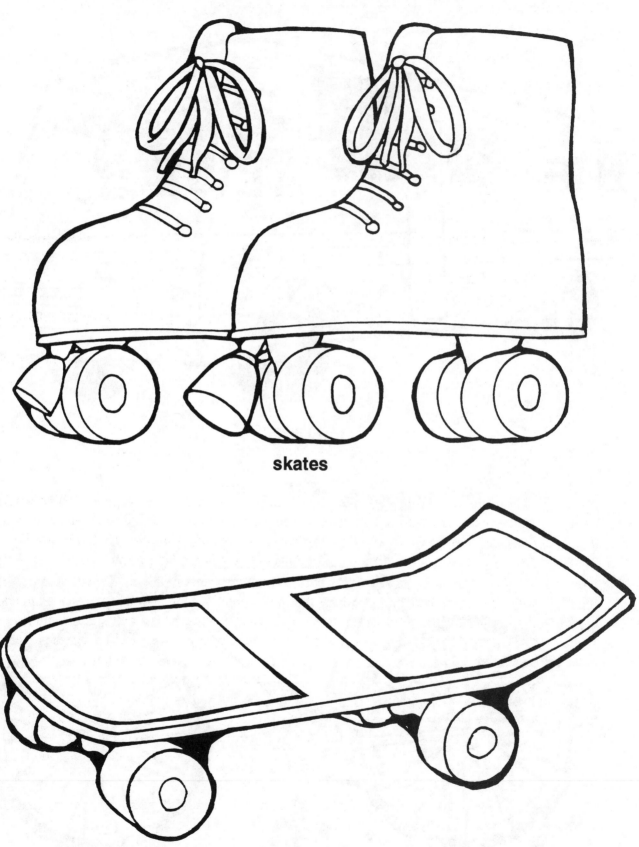

skates

skateboard

Word Relay Race

Purpose: To reinforce the reading/writing vocabulary associated with land travel by focusing on the mural words developed in the previous activity.

Skills: word recognition and identification, word building, listening, and following directions

Materials Per Group: at least three sets of alphabet letters (page 46) and a container for them

Procedures: Begin the activity by having the class review the pictures and words on the mural. Students can point to particular words and call on volunteers to read them aloud. Mention to students that the first kind of travel on land was by foot.

After the review, students can go to their cooperative groups. Have them line up on one side of the room with each group forming a team behind a desk or table. Across the room from each team, on a desk or table, place a container filled with letters. The first student on each team walks across the room, picks a letter, and returns to the group. The student lays the letter on the table in front of the group, and the second student goes to the bowl to get a letter. Each student follows in turn until one of the following happens: (A) a team forms its letters into one of the words on the mural, or (B) the team with the most words at the end of a specified time wins. If you have access to classroom aides, they can be of great assistance in helping the teams find the travel words they need.

To Simplify: Pre-cooperative learners can enjoy this game if they have enough help from older students or parent volunteers. If there is not enough help to go around, have two groups at a time compete while the other groups watch.

To Expand: After advanced students have finished making their words, ask them to use each word orally in a sentence. Vary this activity by asking them to make silly sentences.

Teacher Script:

Today we will begin our activity by reviewing the pictures and words on our mural. Who would like to point to a word on the mural and call on someone to read it? Johnny? *(Johnny goes to the mural, points to a word, and then calls on a volunteer to read the word aloud.)* Great, Maria! Now you can go up and point to a word. *(Continue until all words have been reviewed.)*

Now we will go to our cooperative groups, but this time we won't sit down. We will line up with the rest of our group members on the side of the room behind a desk. Each group is a team, and we are going to play a game. Across the room from each team, there is a bowl full of letters. Watch me walk across the room and pick a letter out of the bowl. As soon as I bring the letter back and lay it on my team's desk, the next person on my team walks across the room to get a letter. While the team waits, we look at the letters. As soon as we see how to make one of the words on the mural from the letters, we lay the letters in order. The first team to form its letters into one of the words on the mural wins. Then we will play another game in which the team with the most words at the end of a specified time wins. Your student and parent aides will help you get started and watch for winners. I will walk around the room to help and answer questions.

Evaluation and Processing: Evaluate this activity by observing the students in action.
Make any appropriate notes on the anecdotal record form, which can later be put in student portfolios. Process with the whole class by having each group read the words it built.

Word Relay Race (cont.)

a	b	c	d	e
f	g	h	i	j
k	l	m	n	o
p	q	r	s	t
u	v	w	x	y
z	a	e	i	o
u	c	r	s	t

Road Trip

Purpose: To provide an opportunity for using oral language skills in both large and small group environments. To communicate with the students' homes about the importance of oral language skills.

Skills: communication (both speaking and listening), visual and auditory memory, comprehension, and application of knowledge

Materials for the Class: "Car Center" (pages 20-21), a nature video, and "Letter to Parents About Oral Language Skills" (page 49, one per student)

Procedures: Begin the activity by having the whole class view a narrated nature video. Try to find one that actually shows the view seen by people riding in a car. Invented (but certainly plausible) titles may include *New England's Autumn Leaves* or *Wildflowers of the Western Deserts*. Tell the students to pretend that they are looking out of a car window and listening to someone who is also riding in the car as he or she tells about the landscape.

Later the same day, when your class is working independently or on projects, have one group at a time come to the car center and sit in the car. One student after another can recreate the scene observed in the video. Ask them to see it in their own "mental movie theater," and to tell about what they are seeing as the narrator does in the video. With very young students, the narrations will be short, so each child can tell the whole thing. Older students will remember more detail, and you may wish to have one begin, another continue, and so on.

To Simplify: Pre-cooperative learners may enjoy imagining and telling about their own road trips. Those who are not ready to share in a group can tell their stories one-on-one to a classroom helper.

To Expand: After advanced students have re-narrated the trip they saw in the video, ask them to decide secretly on another trip, what they might see on that trip, and who will tell what. Join them in the "Car Center." Have them narrate the view seen on their imaginary trip while you try to guess the location to which they have taken you.

Road Trip (cont.)

Teacher Script:

Today you are going to use your imaginations to take a trip. Pretend that you are sitting in a car, looking out the car window, and listening to someone talk about what you are seeing. The video I am going to show is what you see, and the narrator of the video is the person who is talking. Ready? Fasten your seat belts! *(View the video with the students.)*

We will finish this activity later today. Close your eyes for a minute and remember what you saw and heard. Later, I will call one group at a time to come to the car center and to sit in the car.

(Later.) Will group three please come to the car center and sit in the car? Now you are going to retell the imaginary road trip you took earlier in the day. Close your eyes; remember what you saw and what you heard. See it in your own "mental movie theater," and try to hear what the narrator said. Then open your eyes and decide who will start. I will stop you in a minute or two and let the next person continue. *(Listen to the students.)*

Good memory skills! Good oral language skills, too. You may go back to your other activities, and I will call the next group.

Evaluation and Processing: Evaluate this activity by comparing the students' oral narrations with your own memory of the video. Use the anecdotal record forms to make notes about an individual student's visual and auditory memory skills. These forms can later be put in student portfolios. Call the whole class together to process this activity. Ask students to think about questions such as these: Which did you remember best, words or pictures? Do you like to learn by listening? by looking? by doing? Have them watch themselves for a few days to see if they can figure out which way they learn best.

Letter to Parents About Oral Language Skills

Copy this letter and send it home with your students to encourage parents to pay attention to oral language skills.

Dear Parents,

Oral language skills, both in speaking and listening, are very important in our curriculum this year. Please help your child to develop and practice these skills at home by trying some of the following suggestions:

1. Ask your child to tell you the most interesting thing he/she learned at school today. Why was it the most interesting?

2. When your child comes home from a movie, ask him/her to tell you the plot.

3. Watch a television show with your child. When it is over, ask him/her to give you a summary of the story. Compare his/her summary with the storyline you remember.

4. When you give your child important directions, ask him/her to repeat them to you. Then ask for a translation into his/her own words.

5. Watch a nature show on TV with your child, turning the sound off. Ask your child to describe what he/she saw.

6. Listen to your child answer the telephone. Help him/her to develop good telephone speaking habits.

7. Ask your child to avoid slang when speaking to adults. It is important to use oral language appropriate to the particular audience.

Thanks for helping. The very best students are the ones who have interested and involved parents—like you!

Sincerely yours,

_____

Sounds of the Highway

Purpose: To become aware of any sounds associated with highway travel. To create a poem based on sounds. To provide opportunities for sharing ideas in a group and supporting the ideas of others. To learn to use visual art as a complement to language.

Skills: communication (both oral and written), knowledge of parts of speech, group cooperation, and high-order thinking skills (application and synthesis)

Materials Per Group: "Car Center" (pages 20-21), tape recorder(s), general art supplies, poster board, "Write a Sound Poem" (page 52, one per student), and "Parent Letter on Recording Highway Sounds" (page 53, one per student)

Procedures: Begin the activity by having the whole class talk about the sounds they might expect to hear when driving in a car on the highway. Write the sounds on the board as the students brainstorm. You might get suggestions like horns, squealing brakes, car alarms, sirens, the swoosh of cars passing, and so on.

Tell the students that they will do two things with these sounds: write a poem about one of them and record them to make a sound-effects tape for the car center. (If you teach in an urban school, you may be able to record highway sounds right from your playground. If not, ask for parent help in adding to the recording. A letter explaining the project and asking for help appears on page 53.) Students will be writing their poems in their cooperative groups.

When students go to their groups, have them work from the blackline master on page 52, with parent or student help if possible. When all the poems are complete, reassemble as a whole class. A student spokesperson from each group can read his or her group's poem aloud to the class. Encourage applause.

If you take everything home with you, you can letter the poems on the poster boards, ready for the groups to illustrate the following day. Or perhaps a parent helper will volunteer to do this for you. When everything is complete, put the poem posters up on a wall near the car center and put a tape recorder containing the sound tape inside the car center. Students can push the play button when they sit in the car. Parents will love this at Open House!

To Simplify: Pre-cooperative learners (together with pre-readers and pre-writers) can develop their poems orally while a group helper writes them down. The helper can also read the poems aloud to the class.

Sounds of the Highway (cont.)

To Expand: Advanced students may want to write more poems individually. Have them copy their completed poems on good paper and illustrate them. Bind these poems together and add the resulting book of sound poems to your classroom library.

Teacher Script:

Today we are going to talk about the sounds we might expect to hear when driving in a car on the highway. Raise your hand when you think of a sound, and when you tell it to me, I will write it on the board. *(Listen for student input.)*

We are going to do two things with these sounds: write a poem about one of them, and record as many as we can to make a sound-effects tape for the car center. *(At this point, you will say either, "We will go out on the playground this afternoon and start to record," or "I will send a letter home today to see if someone's parents will help us to do this.")*

Now, let's go to your cooperative groups and begin to write. Work through the poem form I am giving you. Your group helper will work with you. When your group poem is finished, choose someone who will be ready to read it aloud to the class. We will have them written on a big poster board for you to illustrate in your groups tomorrow.

Evaluation and Processing: Evaluate this activity by spending time with each group and watching the students work together. Use anecdotal records to make notes to place in the portfolios of individual students. Process as a whole class by appreciating and enjoying the sound poems. If you have time, talk some more about the recording and how it will be used.

Sounds of the Highway (cont.)

Make copies of the poem form below for the cooperative groups to use. Extra ones will come in handy for groups who make false starts or want to recopy their work.

Write a Sound Poem

There are many ways to write poems that follow a pattern. Some use a certain number of syllables, words, or lines. Some use particular parts of speech. Some make a shape or a picture. This poem will be a kind of cinquain. A cinquain is a five-line poem with different kinds of words in each line. The kind of cinquain we are going to write calls for a pattern like this:

- Name of the sound
- 2 words describing the sound
- 3 verbs ending in "ing"
- Phrase telling what the sound makes people do
- Another word for the sound

Here is a sample written for you to look at:

Horn
Loud, clear
Tooting, blaring, blasting
Makes us stop and look
Honk!

Now you try it on the lines below.

_____
(Name of the sound)

_____
(2 words describing the sound)

_____
(3 verbs ending in "ing")

_____
(Phrase telling what the sound makes people do)

_____
(Another word for the sound)

Parent Letter on Recording Highway Sounds

Make copies of this letter to send home if you need help recording highway sounds.

Dear Parents,

As one of our cooperative language arts activities, we are discussing the sounds associated with vehicles driven on the highway. These include honking horns, squealing brakes, backfiring motors, swooshing cars, and many more. We want to bring these sounds to the classroom for our "car center."

We need volunteer parents to make tape recordings of sounds from the highway. We have recording equipment here at the school to borrow. Except for the first volunteer, you will be adding to a tape in progress. It will be all set for you, and you will simply have to push the record button. When you have recorded a sampling of sounds, you will just push the stop button, and the next person will go on from there. We will put a sign on the tape recorder to remind you not to rewind.

The resulting sound-effects tape, "Sounds of the Highway," will be on display in our car center during Open House.

If you can help us, please fill out the form at the bottom of this page and send it back with your child.

Sincerely yours,

_____

- -

I can help record highway sounds for the class.

_____ Please send home the tape recorder with _____.

_____ I will stop by and pick up the tape recorder.

_____
Parent signature

Safety First

Purpose: To promote awareness of and interest in bike safety.

Skills: reading comprehension, writing for a purpose, artistic expression, the ability to work in a group, and high-order thinking skills (application and synthesis)

Materials Per Group: Newspaper clippings about bike safety, bike helmets, the laws affecting bicycle riders, "Poster Guidelines" (page 56), a poster board, art supplies (such as pencils, art gum erasers, poster paint, and brushes), and "Sponsor Letter" (page 57, one per applicable local merchant)

Procedures: Ahead of time, arrange for a contest judge and prize donors by sending out the "Sponsor Letter." Also, fill in the missing information in the "Poster Guidelines" before duplicating them for the children.

Begin the activity with a whole-class discussion on bike helmets (now required by law in some states). Determine if there is a law in your state requiring the wearing of helmets.

Tell the students their homework assignment for the whole week will be to check the newspaper for articles about bike safety, bike laws, etc. Show newspaper clippings of this kind that you have collected, and tell the students that there will be newspapers in class for those who do not get one at home. When the students bring in clippings, have them read them aloud to the class (or give them to you to read aloud) and post them on a special bulletin board. This part of the activity can go on for a week or more, allowing students to build a knowledge base and develop an opinion about bike helmets and safety.

When students are ready to design bike safety posters, tell them they will be making one per group. There will be a contest to choose the very best one. When they go to their groups, give each one a copy of the "Poster Guidelines." Have them discuss their ideas and come to an agreement about their slogan and art work. They should check both slogan and art work with you or another adult before beginning. Then have them make several small trial drawings on paper before lightly sketching their idea on the poster board in pencil. They should not apply paint until they are happy with their ideas and sketches.

To Simplify: Give pre-cooperative learners a few ready-made slogans from which to choose. Have helpers make the pencil sketches on the poster board and guide the hands of the artists when painting.

To Expand: Advanced students can prepare a speech to give when presenting their posters at an assembly or as a traveling exhibit for other classes.

Safety First (cont.)

Teacher Script:

What do you know about bike helmets? Are they required by law in this state? Raise your hand if you know. This week we are going to learn about things like that. Your homework assignment for the whole week will be to check the newspaper for articles about bike safety, bike laws, or anything about bikes. Here are some newspaper clippings that I have collected to share with you. There will be newspapers in class for those who do not get one at home. When you bring in clippings, you may read them aloud to the class and post them on a special bulletin board.

(Go on to the second part of the activity after about a week.) We now are ready to create bike safety posters. You will be making one per group, and there will be a contest to choose the very best one. Read your copy of the "Poster Guidelines." *(Helpers may read to groups.)* Discuss your ideas and come to an agreement about your slogan and art work. Check both your slogan and art work with me or another adult before beginning. Make several small trial drawings on paper before lightly sketching your idea on the poster board in pencil. Do not apply paint until you are happy with your ideas and sketches. Ask your parent or student volunteer for any help you need. I will walk around the room to help and answer questions.

Evaluation and Processing: Evaluate this activity by spending time with each group
and watching the students work together. Have the posters judged by an outsider, and award prizes. Use the anecdotal records to make notes to place in the portfolios of individual students. Process as a whole class by appreciating and enjoying the posters. Plan to share your completed product with other classes.

Poster Guidelines

The slogan on the poster should be...

- Short

- Easy to Remember

The art work on the poster should be...

- Simple

- Big

- Brightly Colored

- Relevant (have something to do with the slogan)

The rules for the poster contest are...

- Subject: _____

- Size: _____

- Information Requested: _____

       _____

- Due Date: _____

Remember to follow the rules exactly!

Sponsor Letter

If merchants in the neighborhood of your school are friendly and supportive, you might want to send this letter (especially to a store that sells sporting goods and biking gear). If you are reluctant or if your school or district has a rule against this, your school's parent organization may want to help you. The police department is always a good source for contest judges.

Dear Neighborhood Merchant,

I am a teacher in your neighborhood school. My class is studying bike safety with a heavy emphasis on wearing bike helmets. We are making posters and having a poster contest, and we wonder if you would be willing to help.

We will need a judge for our poster contest. Would you like to be a judge? We also need one or more prizes for our poster contest, and I am hoping to offer a bike helmet as first prize. Is it possible for you to donate such a prize?

In return, we will be happy to lend you our posters to display in your store for several weeks. We will also tell everyone how you helped our class!

Please let us know if you want to help.

Sincerely yours,

_____

The Golden Spike

Purpose: To write a personal or friendly letter.

Skills: reading, writing, beginning research, listening, teamwork, and following directions

Materials Per Group: "Historical Background" (page 59), "U.S. Map" (page 60), "The Friendly Letter" (page 61, one per student), an encyclopedia and other reference books, and pens or pencils

Procedures: Begin the activity by introducing the idea of research with the "Historical Background" and "U.S. Map" blackline masters. Explain to the students that their cooperative groups will be going to the library with a parent volunteer who will show them how to look up the answers. Each group must be in agreement about their answers.

After completing this research experience, students will pretend that they were on the spot when the transcontinental railroad was completed. They will write a letter home telling about the experience. (Use "The Friendly Letter" master.) The last step will be to read their group letters aloud to the rest of the class.

To Simplify: Pre-cooperative learners will enjoy hearing a story about trains read aloud. They can follow up on this by drawing a picture of a train. They also can make a statement about their train picture to a helper who will write it on the picture, and they can share their pictures with the class.

To Expand: Advanced beginners might enjoy a chance to role play the experiences of people riding the early trains. Have them practice their skit and perform it for the class.

Teacher Script:

Today we are going to learn how to do research. Research is finding information and answers to questions by looking in books. These two worksheets will help you learn how.

Your cooperative groups will be going to the library with parent volunteers who will show you how to look up the answers. Each group must agree that the answers are correct.

When you finish doing research, you will know enough to pretend that you were on the spot when the transcontinental railroad was completed. Then you will write a letter home telling about the experience. When all the letters are finished, you will read yours to the other members of your group. Finally, we will make a book out of the letters and put it in our classroom library.

Evaluation and Processing: Evaluate not only the process of this activity, but also the products: the worksheet and the writing sample. Make any appropriate notes on the anecdotal records which can later be put in student portfolios. Process with groups by asking them about the letters they wrote and heard. Were they interesting? Did they seem real? Did the students learn anything from the activity? What?

Group name_____

Historical Background

Look in encyclopedias and other reference books to fill in the blanks.

The United States stretches from the _____ Ocean to the
_____Ocean. The transcontinental railway began in the city of
_____on the east coast and in the city of _____on
the west coast.

The two parts of this railway finally met near _____ in the year
_____. When they met, a _____was driven.

People suffered many hardships while laying track for the railway. It was cold in
the high snowy mountains and hot on the plains. But when the railway was
completed, it seemed to hold this big country together from one ocean to the
other.

Group name _____

U.S. Map

Look in encyclopedias and other reference books. Then draw in the route of the transcontinental railway. Be sure to mark any important cities.

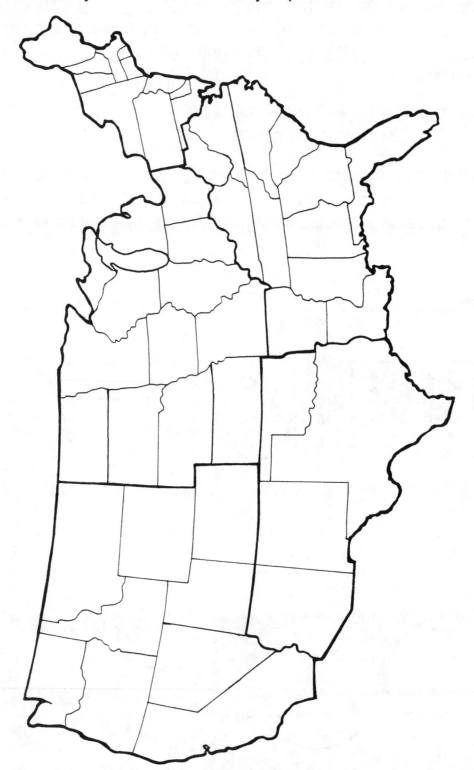

60

Group name_____

The Friendly Letter

Writing Situation: You have been working on the transcontinental railway for a couple of years without getting home to see your family. Now, today, it is finished!

Directions for Writing: Write a letter home telling your family about the day. Use your best writing skills. You do not want them to think you forgot what you learned in school.

_____

_____

_____

_____

_____

_____

_____

_____

_____

_____

_____

_____

_____

_____

Cooperation by Land

Fantasy Field Trip

Purpose: To imagine and write about a fantasy trip.

Skills: imagination, writing, ability to differentiate between fact and fantasy, oral language skills, and cooperative learning skills

Materials Per Group: "Bus Story Cover" (page 63), "Bus Story Pages" (page 64, duplicated as many times as necessary), and assorted writing and drawing materials

Procedures: Begin the activity by discussing buses and field trips. If most children have gone on field trips, ask them to share their experiences. Establish the fact that they went to real places. Then talk about what fun it would be to go on a fantasy field trip to a make-believe place.

When the students meet with their groups, they will continue their discussion of fantasy field trips. Each group will then decide on its own place to go, and the students in each group will write about it. Students will then copy their stories on the bus paper and color the special cover. They can share their stories with the other groups.

To Simplify: Pre-cooperative learners can tell their stories to helpers who will transcribe them.

To Expand: Advanced students can continue by discussing real field trip possibilities, brainstorming future destinations, and making a list of suggestions and reasons for those suggestions.

Teacher Script:

Today we are going to talk about a special, fun kind of field trip. How many of you have gone on a field trip? How many of you rode on a bus? Where did you go? Raise your hands, and I will call on you. *(Students share their experiences.)*

A lot of you went to different places, but in one way, all the places were the same. They were all real places. What if I told you I went to a magic forest? Would that be real? Of course not. It would be make-believe or pretend. Today you are going to plan and write about make-believe field trips!

When you get to your groups, talk some more about make-believe field trips. Then, decide where you as a group would like to go. Once you have decided, you will write about it. Use scratch paper for your first draft and ask for help if you need it. When your story is finished, copy it onto the special bus paper and color the cover. When everyone is finished, each group will choose one person to read the story aloud to the other groups.

I will walk around the room and help.

Evaluation and Processing: Evaluate each student's understanding of real and make-believe and his/her ability to function in a group. Make any appropriate notes on the anecdotal record, and store the records in their portfolios. Process with groups by asking them what they liked best about the activity. Would they do anything differently if they did it again?

Bus Story Cover

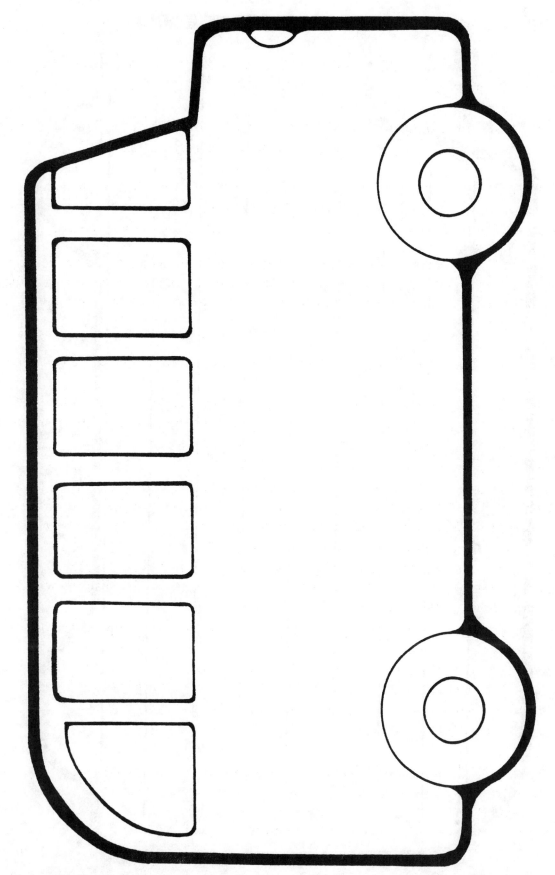

Bus Story Pages

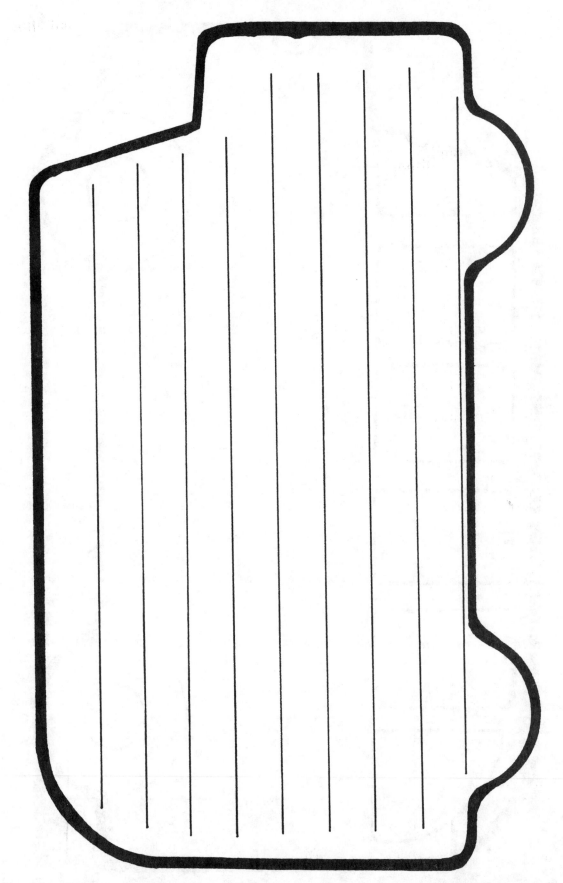

On the Road with Venn Diagrams

Purpose: To learn to read information from a Venn diagram.

Skills: oral language and high-order thinking (application and synthesis)

Materials Per Group: "Venn Diagram Form" (page 66), writing materials, two or more pieces of string about 3 feet (1 meter) long, and small blocks of different shapes and colors

Procedures: Make a Venn diagram by drawing two overlapping circles on the chalkboard. Write the subject "water transportation" under the left circle and "land transportation" under the right. Ask the students to name modes of each transportation. Any that fit both categories can be written in the middle section where the circles overlap. Individual modes can be written in the individual circles.

After you have modeled Venn diagrams, the groups can practice making their own diagrams. Give them the string and some blocks. They can tie the string into circles and group the blocks according to their shared attributes.

Next, give the groups the topics "boy's names" and "girl's names." Have them do a Venn diagram with these topics. Using the provided form, they can write names in the circles, placing names that can be either boy's or girl's in the overlapping part. If they would like, they can use the names from the students in class.

To Simplify: Pre-cooperative learners can simply sort the blocks according to various attributes and explain their reasoning to a parent helper.

To Expand: Students can make up mathematical word problems to test one another. For example, if a truck is carrying fifteen boxes to the school, a train is carrying ten boxes, and five boxes are coming part way by train and part way by truck, what would the diagram showing this look like?

Teacher Script:

Today we are going to read something other than words. Watch. *(Draw and label the Venn diagram)* We will write things that belong only to the first group over here. We will write things that belong only to the second group over here. We will write things that belong to both groups in the middle. *(Allow time for activity.)*

Now, I want you to join your groups. As a group, you will make a diagram like this, called a Venn diagram, out of string. I will also give you some blocks. Take the blocks and think of two different groups to which they can belong. Group them in the string Venn diagram. *(Allow time for activity.)*

Now, take your Venn diagram paper and complete it in this way. Label the left circle "boy names" and label the right circle "girl names." Put names that belong to both groups in the middle. Use the names of the people in this class. I will walk around the room and help.

Evaluation and Processing:

Evaluate the students' ability to sort and categorize. Make any appropriate notes on the anecdotal records. Process with the groups by asking them what they liked best about the activity. Would they do anything differently if they did it again?

Group name_____

Venn Diagram Form

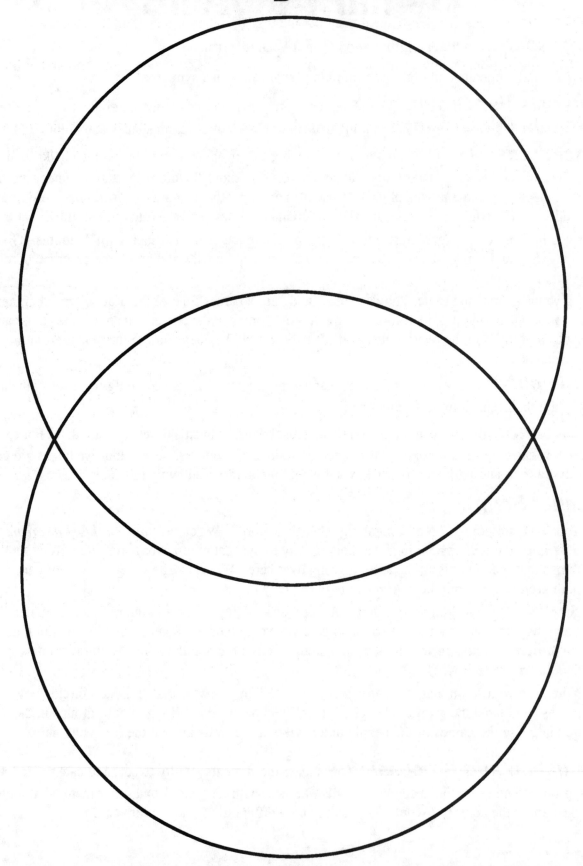

Make-Believe Transportation

Purpose: To create a make-believe form of land transportation and explain it to the class.

Skills: imagination, creativity, team work, discussion, art, decision making, and oral and written language skills

Materials Per Group: "Planning Worksheet" (page 69), "Transportation Design" (page 70), and assorted art supplies and materials for building transportation models (or poster paper and art supplies to draw and color the design)

Procedures: Begin this activity by recapping the various modes of transportation that have been studied in the classroom so far. Ask the children to share what they have learned about bikes, cars, trains, buses, and trucks. Then ask them to think about what kind of make-believe land transportation they would invent if they could create anything they wanted to, no matter how strange or impossible it seemed.

Have the students move into their groups, and with the help of any available student or parent volunteers, they can talk about the kind of land transportation they would invent if they could make anything they wanted. Use the "Planning Worksheet" to make notes.

Next, have each group sketch the imaginary transportation it designs. The groups can then write a brief description of the transportation and what makes it special.

Finally, ask the groups to build a small model of their design (or have them draw and color it in detail on the poster paper). When the project is complete, each group can choose a member to explain the transportation design to the class.

To Simplify: Have the groups simply discuss and sketch their imaginary form of transportation.

To Expand: Have each group prepare a round-robin story (in which each member makes up a sentence) to go with their picture. Use these stories and pictures for a colorful bulletin board display.

Make-Believe Transportation (cont.)

Teacher Script:

Today, we are going to talk about all the different kinds of land transportation we have learned about. Let's see if we can name them all. I'll write them on the board as you say them so that we can all look at them. *(Do so. Also, discuss the various features of each mode of transportation.)*

Now, let's get ready to be creative and use our imaginations! Today, we are going to work in groups to design a make-believe land transportation. Who can tell me what I mean by "make-believe"? *(Listen and discuss.)*

So, we all understand "make-believe." Now, I want you to think about what kind of transportation you would make if you could make anything you want. Let your imaginations go. Don't worry if it seems too strange or impossible.

Let's get together in our groups to brainstorm for an imaginary form of transportation. Make notes on the worksheet I will give you. I'll walk around the room to help. After you have thought about your transportation, sketch it on the other sheet I will give you.

When your sketch is complete, your group will build a small model of it using these materials. *(Or, each group will draw and color the design on this poster paper.)* Afterwards, each group will share its design with the other groups. One person can volunteer to tell the class about it.

Evaluation and Processing: Evaluate this activity by using the anecdotal records and spending time with each group to watch its imaginative process. Be sure to make notes on each individual student's form, and date these for the portfolios. Also, use this form to note presentation skills.

Group name_____

Planning Worksheet

The name of our make-believe transportation is_____.

Here are the special things our transportation will do:

1. _____

2. _____

3. _____

4. _____

5. _____

6. _____

7. _____

8. _____

9. _____

10. _____

Group name_____

Transportation Design

Work together to make a sketch of your make-believe form of transportation. Label your sketch with the name of your transportation.

_____

(name)

Setting the Scene: Sea Mural

Purpose: To build vocabulary associated with sea travel through whole-class and cooperative group activity, thereby improving cooperative group skills.

Skills: word identification, reading comprehension, writing of upper and lower case letters, oral communication (both speaking and listening), decision making, and art

Materials for the Class: mural already established (page 34), drawing paper, pre-cut strips for labels, old magazines, pencils, markers and other coloring materials, scissors, staplers, and "Sea Travel Pictures" (pages 73-77)

Procedures: Begin the activity with a whole-class discussion in which students think of and name various kinds of sea transportation, while you write the words on the chalkboard. Be sure to include the modes of transportation included on pages 73-77. When students are ready to go to their cooperative groups, assign one or more types of transportation to each group. Students work together to draw (or use the provided pictures), color, and cut out examples of their type(s) of transportation, mounting them on the sea section of the mural and labeling them. They may use the words you wrote on the board during the whole-group discussion to verify their spelling. If possible, have each group work with an older student or parent volunteer.

To Simplify: For pre-cooperative learners, provide pictures cut from magazines or from pages 73-77 and pre-made labels. Have students work in their groups to match the pictures and labels. When all agree that the pictures and labels are correctly matched, students may mount them on the mural. Older students and parent volunteers will be very helpful here.

To Expand: After advanced students have finished their pictures and labels and have mounted them on the mural, they may continue to work on their travel dictionaries. These dictionaries can be kept in notebooks or on sheets of paper fastened together with brads or yarn. (See "Travel Dictionary" on page 37.) Each page should have a letter of the alphabet at the top. Students will write travel words on the appropriate pages and use them as a spelling help for their writing activities. Students who want to may add definitions and illustrations. These dictionaries will be ongoing through the year, and they can be stored in the student's portfolios and then displayed during a culminating activity party or as part of an open house event.

Setting the Scene: Sea Mural (cont.)

Teacher Script:

Today we are going to talk some more about being travelers. We will meet first as a large group and then move into our cooperative learning groups.

Look at the bulletin board. We will be working on the next part of our mural. Today we will talk about sea travel. Raise your hand as soon as you think of a way to travel on the sea. *(Teacher accepts all suggestions and prints the words on the chalkboard.)* If that list names every kind of sea travel you can think of, we are ready for the next part of the activity.

Each small group will have a kind of sea travel for its own. Some of you may need to do more than one kind. *(Teacher makes assignments.)* You can color the pictures that I will give you, cut pictures out of magazines, or draw your own. Talk to the other members of your group to plan what you are doing. For example, Group 2 is responsible for small boats. The students in the group will want to decide who will make rowboats and who will make other kinds of boats. When your pictures are finished, you will take a strip of paper *(teacher displays)* and write the name of your picture on it. Then you will put your picture and its name in a good place on the mural. The parent or student aide in your group can help you if you need it. I will walk around the room to help and answer questions.

Evaluation and Processing: Evaluate this activity by spending time with each group, listening to its discussion, and watching its creation of a product. (Have copies of the anecdotal records handy.) Process the activity with the whole class by looking at and admiring the mural. Have students tell what they liked best about the activity and what they would still like to do. Allow interested, motivated students to add to the mural as an extra-credit homework assignment.

Sea Travel Pictures

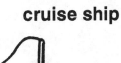

cruise ship

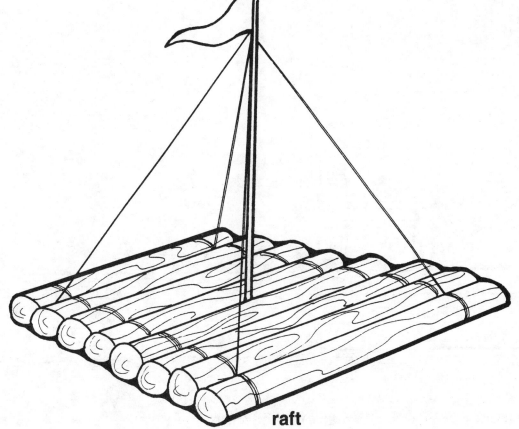

raft

Sea Travel Pictures (cont.)

steamboat

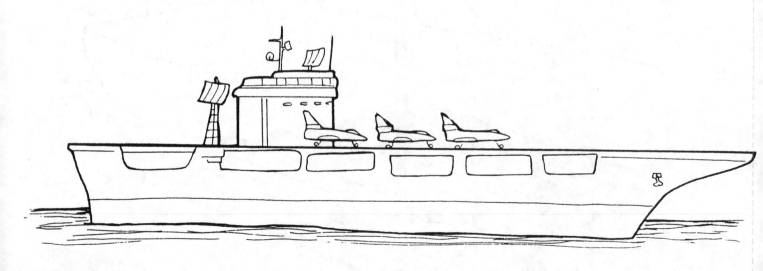

aircraft carrier

Sea Travel Pictures (cont.)

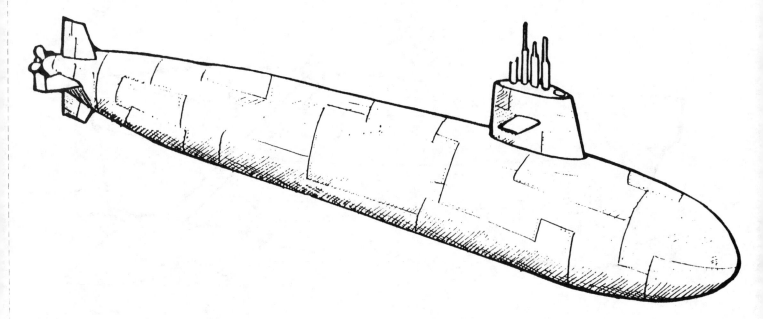

submarine

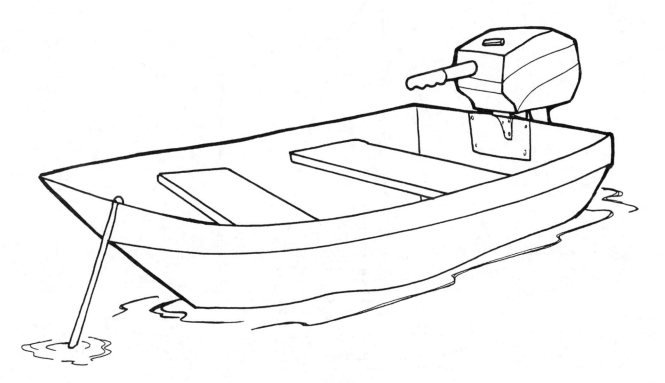

motorboat

Sea Travel Pictures (cont.)

rowboat

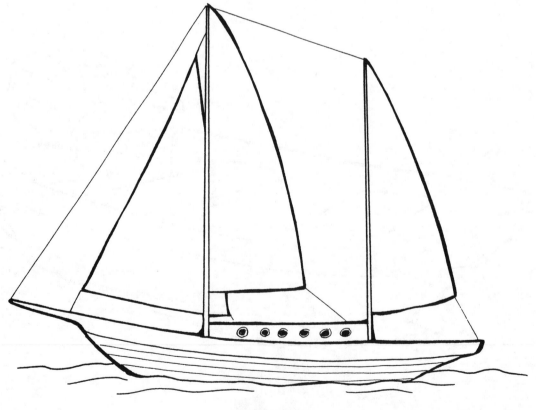

sailboat

Sea Travel Pictures (cont.)

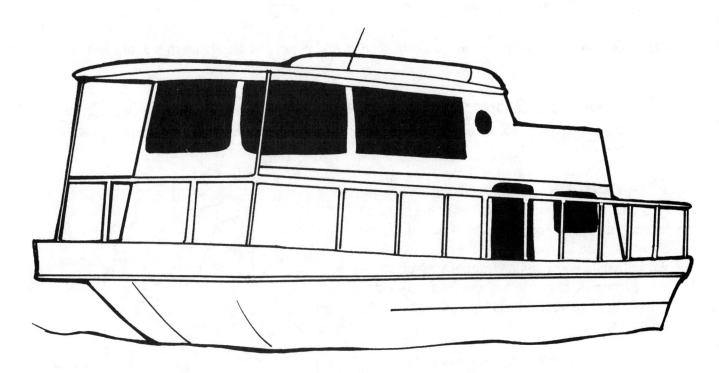

houseboat

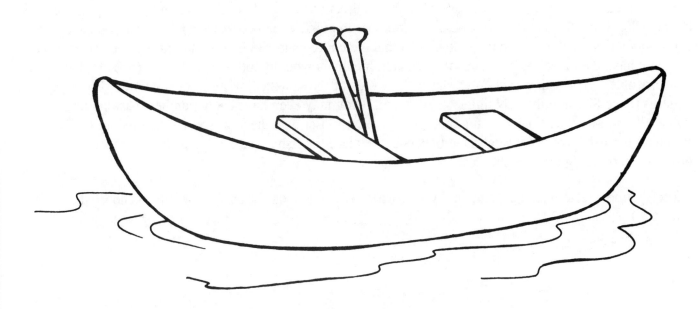

canoe

Go Fish

Purpose: To construct sentences in proper syntactical order.

Skills: reading, writing, decision making, team work, logic, and the ability to identify parts of speech

Materials Per Group: one two-foot (60 cm) dowel or yardstick, string or yarn, one bucket, brads, one large paper clip, "Fishy Sentences" (page 81), "Fish Pattern" (page 82), paper, and a pen or pencil

Procedures: Students work together to play "Go Fish," a sentence construction game. Begin the activity by conducting a whole-class discussion about the parts of speech. Base this discussion on the skill and understanding level of your class. Some teachers may wish to focus on nouns and verbs while others will include adjectives, pronouns, etc.

Explain to the students that they will be playing a fun game that will help them learn to construct proper sentences. Model the idea of a simple sentence by diagraming several simple sentences on the board. Leave this board display available for students to look at during the activity.

Give each team of students all necessary materials. Directions for making the fish and fishing pole are on page 80. Have the teams each choose one member to pick a sentence from page 81. (If you have classroom aides, you may have them do this so that the entire team can interact to unravel the sentence; or if you have the time, you can do this.) All team members who do not choose the sentence are the "fisherpeople." The sentence chooser places the words of the sentence, written separately on fish patterns (page 82) onto the fishing line of the team. (You may even have each member "cast the line" while the chooser places one fish at a time on it.) The chooser puts the words in an incorrect order. When all the fish have been caught, the fishers try to place the fishy words in their proper sentence order by rearranging them on the line.

(**Note:** You may also play this game in reverse, whereby one person fishes and the others choose the sentence.)

Go Fish (cont.)

To Simplify: Have children work together in teams to create fishy words. Omit the fishing pole game and have children pull fishy words from a bucket, matching them to the sentences on the fishy sentence worksheet (page 81).

To Expand: Have children play "Go Fish," but instead of using the provided sentences, they can write their own. See who can write the longest sentence, the shortest sentence, etc.

Teacher Script: Today we are going to play a fun game that will help us learn to write correct sentences. But first, let's talk a little bit about sentences. What do we know already? *(Class discussion about the parts of speech.)*

Now we are going to learn to play a game called "Go Fish." I will demonstrate how this game works. First, let's look at this sentence: "I want to go fishing." I need some volunteers to help me. Let's pretend Billy, Alex, and Sheila don't know that this is the sentence I have chosen. First they fish for the words. I will attach a word to their line every time one of them fishes, until all of the words (fish) have been placed on the line. I will be very careful not to put the words in the right order. My team members will need to look at all the words on the line, and through cooperation, figure out the right order and put them that way. If they have trouble, the "fish" can help them by moving around in different orders until they make sense. Now, let's all get a pole, a bucket of fishy words, and try this in our groups. I will give each group a worksheet that has sentences from which to choose. I will walk around the room and help you get started. Each group that solves all of its sentences will get a surprise.

Evaluation and Processing: Evaluate individual student groups during the game-playing process. Use the anecdotal records and remember to date each entry for individual student portfolios. Process the activity with your whole class by having student groups share about the experience and discuss which sentences were the easiest, the most difficult, etc.

How to Prepare for Go Fish

Making Fishy Words

Copy the fish pattern (page 82) onto card stock or heavy card paper. You will need many copies so that every team has a fish for every word of the sentences on page 81. Write one word from the sentences per fish. Keep the words from each set of sentences separate so that every team has one complete set. Poke holes through the fish where indicated on the pattern in order to affix brads. Attach one brad at the fish's nose, but leave the hole at the fish's tail empty.

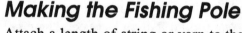

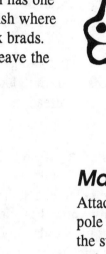

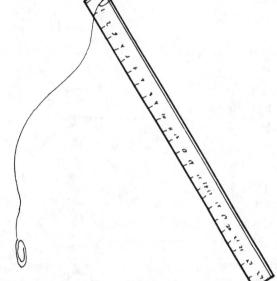

Making the Fishing Pole

Attach a length of string or yarn to the end of a pole or yardstick. (A yardstick works well because the string can be pulled through the hole in the end and secured easily.) Make the string approximately the same length as the pole. At the end of the string, attach a paperclip "hook."

Setting Up the Game

Provide each team with a bucket, fishing pole, and the prepared fishy words. See the procedures on page 78 for the rules of play. Fish can be attached to the fishing line and to one another as illustrated.

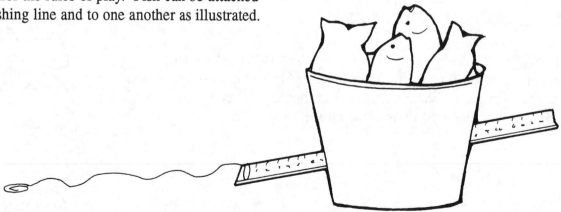

Fishy Sentences

Write each word of the sentences below on a fish pattern (page 82). Provide students with this list so that they have a guideline when unscrambling their sentences.

I want to go fishing.

I am going fishing today.

I got wet.

I have a fishing pole.

I caught a fish!

I put the fish back.

Fishing is fun for me.

You like to fish.

The fish swim quickly.

I will catch a fish.

Fish Pattern

See directions on page 80.

Underwater Adventure

Purpose: To develop auditory and visual memory skills by taking, and then remembering and drawing, an imaginary submarine voyage.

Skills: auditory and visual memory, listening, communication, writing, reading, and art

Materials Per Group: video, movie, or television program with underwater sea footage (such as a Jacques Cousteau film), art supplies (including crayons and watercolors), a large sheet of butcher paper, and "Underwater Word List" (page 85)

Procedures: Students will take an imaginary underwater journey by watching the video or film, and then they will discuss it in their cooperative groups. Afterwards, they can work together to make a crayon and watercolor underwater picture.

To make the picture, have the children draw underwater objects using crayons, and then have them paint over their entire picture with a weak watercolor mixture.

When the groups have completed their pictures (set two days aside for this activity so the pictures can dry thoroughly), have them exchange them. They can use the "Underwater Word List" form to write the names of the things they see in the picture. (Or, individual groups can make word lists using their own picture.)

After the groups have completed their word lists, they can meet with the group that drew the picture. Have them discuss the words they wrote on their word lists and decide with the other group whether or not they missed anything. End the activity by giving children the opportunity to share about their own picture and how well the other group understood what was drawn.

To Simplify: Have beginning students draw individual pictures of an underwater scene and trade them with a partner. They can then discuss what they see in their partner's picture, naming the objects. Then have students work with a student helper or parent to complete an underwater word list.

To Expand: Have student groups use their underwater word lists to write a short story or one sentence for each word on the list.

Underwater Adventure (cont.)

Teacher Script:

Today we are going to have an underwater sea adventure. We are going to watch this underwater video and pretend we are looking at the sea from inside a submarine.

First, let's all look for a minute at our sea mural on the bulletin board. Who would like to show me the submarine? Great! Who can tell me how a submarine is different from other boats and ships? Great!

Now let's all watch the video. Pay special attention to all the plants and animals and other objects you see under the water. *(View video.)*

Now, we are going to work in our groups to make an underwater picture. Before you start, talk it over in your group and see how many things you can remember from the video. Then use your crayons to draw the things you remember. You need to decide who will do which part of the drawing. If you have any trouble deciding, ask me or our classroom aide for help.

After you have finished, paint the blue water over your picture. You will make the paint very thin and watery. *(After the pictures dry, the activity continues.)*

Now, we are going to trade pictures. After your group trades pictures with another group, here is what I would like you to do. Take this worksheet and write the names of the objects or things you see in the picture. *(Model the activity.)* After your group has finished, I would like you to join the group you exchanged pictures with to discuss them. Did they write the names of all of the things in the picture?

When everyone has finished, we will talk about the activity and put all of our wonderful pictures on the board for everyone to see.

Evaluation and Processing: Evaluate individual student performances using the anecdotal records. Process this activity with your whole class by discussing the activity and mounting finished underwater scenes in a bulletin board display.

Group name _____

Underwater Word List

We saw these underwater objects:

1. _____

2. _____

3. _____

4. _____

5. _____

6. _____

7. _____

8. _____

9. _____

10. _____

This is what we liked best about the picture:

_____

_____

_____

_____

_____

_____

_____

_____

Treasure!

Purpose: To create a project cooperatively.

Skills: reading, research, organization, art, and decision making

Materials Per Group: "How to Make a Treasure Chest" (page 87), "Treasure Patterns" (pages 88-90), "A Treasure Story" (page 91), a box with a lid, papier-mâché materials (or flour and salt paste), and appropriate treasure-making supplies (such as glitter, clay, beads, shiny paper and paints, aluminum foil, and so on)

Procedures: The students will work together to research and create their own treasure chest full of treasure. To begin this activity, read "A Treasure Story." Then, have the students select books from the class or school library that tell about treasure, or assist them in locating information about treasure from encyclopedias. Ask the students to discuss the information they found with the class.

Next, have them move into their cooperative groups to create their treasure and their treasure chest. (Make a chest ahead of time to model for the students.) Use the directions and patterns on pages 87-90. (Explain to the students that in this activity they will create their treasure, but in a later one they will hide it and make a map for the rest of the class to use.)

After the students have completed their treasure and treasure chests, give the groups a chance to view each other's finished products.

To Simplify: Omit the research step. Have the students make treasure chests after reading "A Treasure Story." Gather costume jewelry or make the treasure ahead of time and have the groups select treasure for their treasure chests.

To Expand: Omit reading "A Treasure Story" and begin the activity with a detailed research project for each student group.

Teacher Script:

Today, we are going to learn about something really interesting—treasure! We are going to talk about buried treasure and treasure chests, but first I am going to read you a story. Listen as I read to you, and then we will talk about it. *(Read "A Treasure Story!")*

Now, let's talk about treasure. *(Class discussion.)* Has anyone ever seen a treasure chest? Let's all look at the picture on the story page. What kinds of things do you see in the treasure chest? *(Discuss.)*

Now we are all going to make treasure chests. Let's look at the treasure chest I have made. Can anyone tell me how I made it? Good. Now, let's look inside. What do we see? *(Discuss.)*

Each group is going to make a treasure chest, and when we are finished, we are going to hide it and draw a map. *(See "Treasure Hunt!" on pages 92-97.)* I will walk around the room to help you get started.

Evaluation and Processing: Use the anecdotal records to record individual student

performance. Process with your whole class by viewing and discussing the different treasure chests and comparing their contents.

How to Make a Treasure Chest

1. Start with a box and lid.

2. Color or paint them.

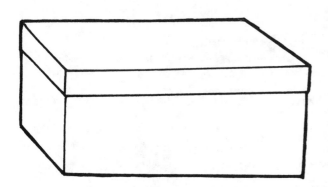

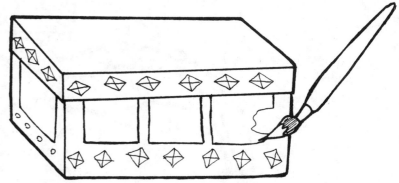

3. Color and cut out a lock from the pattern provided. Glue it onto the box, making sure that you can still open the lid.

4. Make your treasure. You can use the patterns provided.

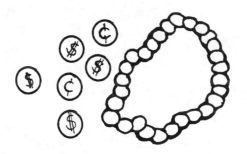

5. Put your treasure in the treasure chest. Close the lid. Now, you have a treasure chest!

Treasure Patterns

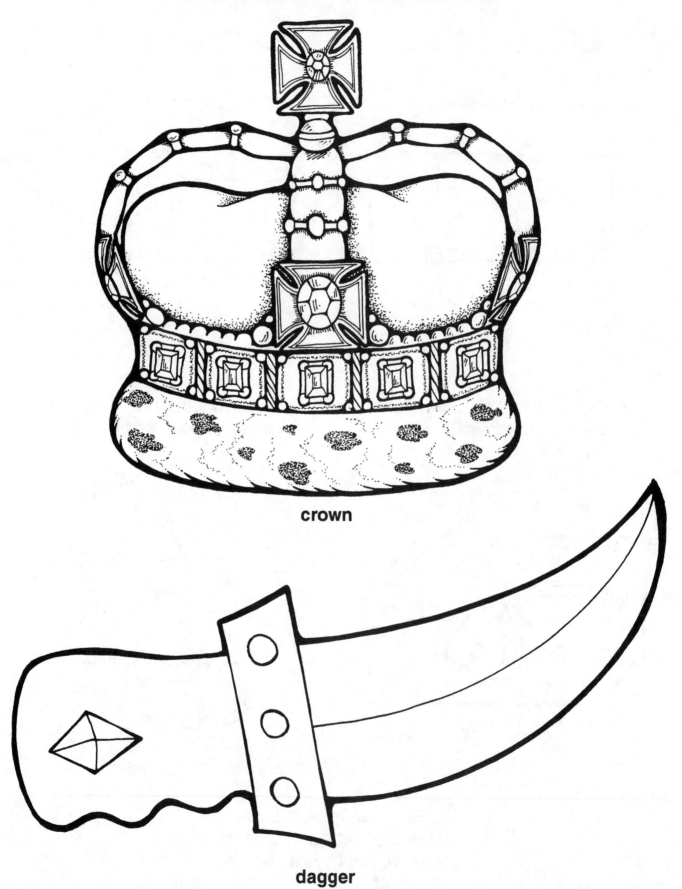

crown

dagger

Treasure Patterns (cont.)

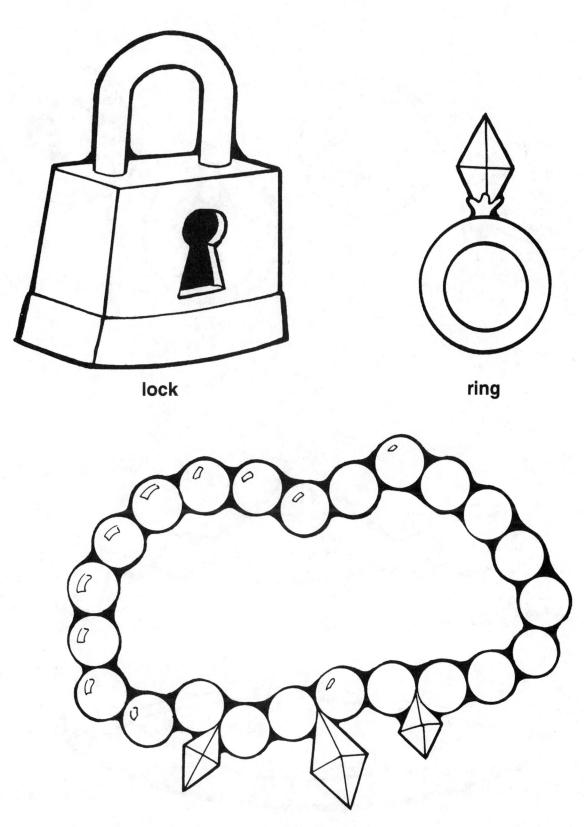

lock

ring

necklace

Treasure Patterns (cont.)

coins

tiara

A Treasure Story

Many years ago, a terrible pirate had a treasure chest. It was full of riches. In his treasure chest he had gold coins, diamonds, jewelry, and other precious things. He buried his treasure so no one would find it, and he made a treasure map.

The terrible pirate never came back to dig up his treasure, so for years and years it has been buried under the ground. Wouldn't it be wonderful if we could find a buried treasure!

Cooperation by Sea

Treasure Hunt!

Purpose: To create an accurate map and directions for finding "buried treasure."

Skills: writing, oral language, sequencing, following written directions, decision making, imagination, and art

Materials Per Group: completed treasure chest (pages 87-90), brown construction paper (or large paper bags cut into large sheets of paper), art supplies, examples of treasure maps from books or other reference materials (optional), "Buried Treasure Clues" (page 94), "Treasure Map" (page 95), "How to Look Like a Pirate" (page 96), and "Eye Patches" (page 97)

Procedures: (Before beginning, note that this activity can be spread out over a week.) Begin by having a whole-class discussion about treasure maps. Share examples from books or other resources. Discuss some reasons why treasure may have been buried and maps made.

Some teachers may wish to begin this activity by creating a model (complete with buried treasure) and having the whole class follow the map to see if they can find the treasure. Others may wish to omit this step, depending on the readiness of the class.

Explain to students that they must have a secret pirate meeting. Break into groups. The students will work together to plan where to hide their treasure chest, and they will make a map and clues for the rest of the class to follow. (Use the "Buried Treasure Clues" and "Treasure Map" masters.) After each group has decided upon its treasure hiding place, the students in the group should meet secretly with the teacher to hide their treasure. (Make sure to keep a personal record of where all treasure chests are hidden!) At this time, discuss with each group its hiding place and some ideas about how they might show it on the map.

To make the map, each group will need two large pieces of brown construction paper and the treasure map pattern on page 95. Have students work together to draw a map that leads to the spot in the classroom where they have hidden their treasure. They should use page 95 as a guide for their own maps.

When the map is complete, each group will decide what clues or directions should be provided on the clue page. These clues should be sequential hints or steps in finding the treasure. Then, spend several days meeting with groups individually while they work on their maps and clues.

Before concluding, follow the directions on pages 96 and 97 for making pirate costumes. When all is complete, end the activity with a treasure hunt and pirate party! Have each team of pirates (dressed accordingly) present their map and clues to the rest of the class. The class will follow the clues to find the treasure. The pirate team will respond as they search, saying, "Warm," or "Cold," as the class gets near or far.

When all the treasure is found, you might host a movie party where students can view *Treasure Island, Swiss Family Robinson*, or another appropriate film. Enjoy cookies, punch, and candy gold coins while you watch!

Treasure Hunt! (cont.)

To Simplify: Have student groups work together to draw a treasure map and explain it orally to the rest of the class. Then follow up with a movie and punch and cookies. (Omit the sequential clues.)

To Expand: Make each treasure clue a riddle, adding to the challenge of the hunt.

Teacher Script:

Today, we are going to begin making our own treasure maps. Later, we will hide our treasure chests and make clues to go along with the maps. On the last day, we will have a treasure hunt, where the rest of the class will look for each group's treasure.

First, I would like you to go to your groups to have a secret pirate meeting. Talk very quietly about where in the room you would like to hide your treasure. Then, after you have decided, I will have a secret meeting with each team of pirates to help them hide their treasure chests in the room. *(Schedule secret meetings, allowing ten to fifteen minutes to help individual student groups.)*

(Later) Now, we are going to make our pirate costumes. *(Model the provided directions.)*

(Final Activity Day) Today we are going to hunt for treasure. *(Have your whole class use clues and treasure maps to hunt for each group's treasure.)* Now that we have found all the treasure, let's watch our pirate movie and have a pirate party!

Student Group Script:

Where would you like to hide your treasure chest? Okay, how do you think you could show that on a map? Let's make a little sketch. Now, if we hide it in the cupboard under the sink, what will be our first hint? Should we start with the front door of the classroom, and make an arrow pointing in? Great. Okay, now go back to your group and draw your map. You can make a practice map first, and then copy it over again if you would like. Then you will write your clues on your clue list. *(Or, the classroom aide will help you to write your clues.)* After we are done, we will hunt for treasures.

Evaluation and Processing: Evaluate individual student performances by using the anecdotal records. Make sure to date them for the individual student portfolios. Process with your whole class by having a whole-class treasure hunt and party!

Group name_____

Buried Treasure Clues

(Fill in only as many clues as you would like.)

1. _____

2. _____

3. _____

4. _____

5. _____

6. _____

7. _____

8. _____

9. _____

10. _____

94

Treasure Map

Use this map as a guideline for drawing your own map on brown paper.

How to Look Like a Pirate

Materials:

- construction paper (brown, black, and assorted other colors)
- thin cardboard or heavy paper
- scissors
- crayons and markers
- kerchiefs or squares of cloth
- newspaper
- glitter and beads (optional)

Dagger Directions:

Use the pattern on page 88. Trace the dagger onto the cardboard or heavy paper. Cut out. Color, or decorate with glitter and beads to make the dagger look jeweled.

Kerchief Directions:

Tie a kerchief or a square of fabric sideways around the neck to resemble a pirate's scarf.

Hat Directions:

1. Make a pirate hat out of newspaper. Cut the newspaper to about 12" x 18" (30 cm x 46 cm).
2. Fold the paper in half to 12" x 9" (30 cm x 23 cm). Keep the fold on top.
3. Fold the upper left and right corners to join in the middle, and then fold in half again.
4. Open the bottom, and then fold up to form the brim.
5. Pull the hat open, color and decorate it if you would like, and wear it. Yo-Ho-Ho!

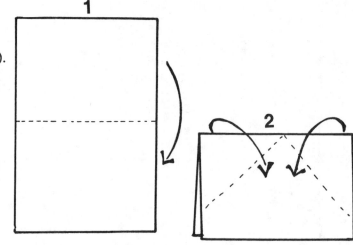

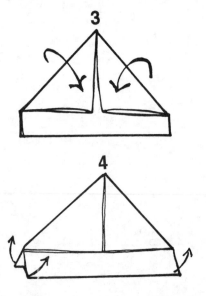

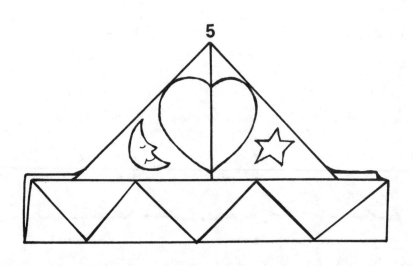

Eye Patches

Trace these patches onto colored paper (black will be the most realistic), or simply color them and cut them out. Cut or punch a small hole in each side. Tie string through each hole in order to tie the patch around your head. (**Note:** These patches go over the right eye.)

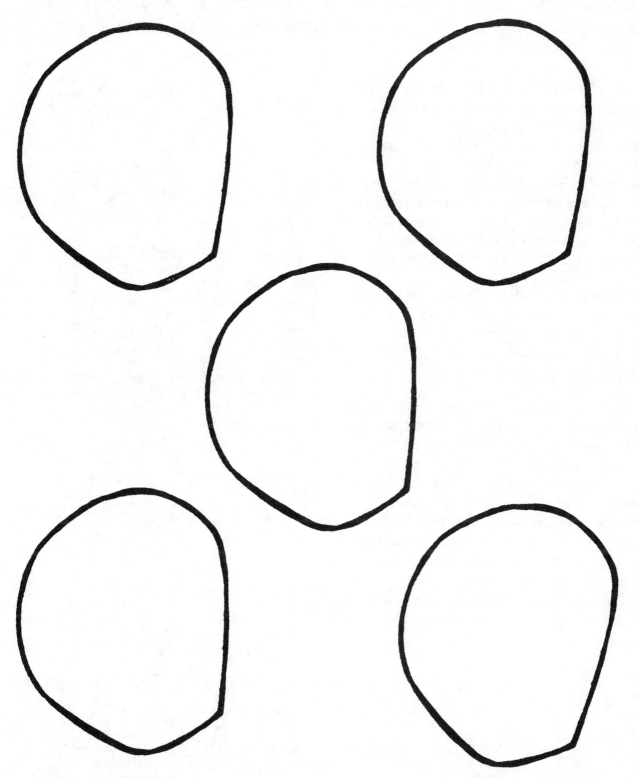

A Fish Tale

Purpose: To create and publish short tales about an imaginary fish.

Skills: writing, reading, imagination, art, memory, communication, and oral language

Materials Per Group: "Fish Tale Pattern" (pages 101-102: one head per group and one tail per student), general writing and art supplies (including paper), "Harry, the Very Smart Fish" (page 100), and the "Boat Center" (pages 19-21)

Procedures: Children go on a make-believe fishing trip and write about an imaginary fish they catch. Begin the activity by holding a class discussion about fishing trips and the trips that students may have taken by boat or ship. Talk about the different kinds of vessels and refer to pages 73-77 for pictures. Have children work in groups to complete an individual imaginary fish. Provide art and writing supplies so that students can use their imaginations to create their fish.

Some teachers may wish to talk about mermaids and other imaginary or make-believe kinds of sea life. Discuss how an imaginary fish can be different from an ordinary fish, and follow up by reading "Harry, The Very Smart Fish."

Explain to students that each student group will go on an imaginary fishing trip in the "Boat Center." Give each group time to plan and have an imaginary adventure in the center. After each group has finished its trip, have the students write individual fish tales, short stories about their adventures. If classroom aides are available, have each group work with an aide. Finish the activity by binding the fish tales from a group into a large display book (page 102). Display all of the books as a bulletin board or as a feature in your reading center if you have one.

A Fish Tale (cont.)

To Simplify: Have students draw an imaginary fish and tell the other members of their group about it. Write each student's description of his/her fish on the "Fish Tale Pattern" (page 102) to display or take home.

To Expand: Have students pose with their catch for a polaroid picture. Use a tape recorder to interview fish catchers, play back the interviews, and discuss.

Teacher Script:

Today, we are going to go on an imaginary fishing trip to catch an imaginary fish. Can anyone tell me what I mean by imaginary? Yes, that's right. I mean pretend.

Before we go on our fishing trip, I would like to read you a story called, "Harry, the Very Smart Fish." *(Read story.)* Harry wasn't like real fish, was he? How was he different? He was imaginary. The writer who wrote this story made up an imaginary fish.

Now, in our cooperative groups we are all going to draw imaginary fish. They can be different from real fish ... just use your imaginations. After we have finished our fish, each group will get to play a fishing trip in the boat center. You can plan out the trip you would like to take, and then have fun pretending.

Once your group has taken its trip, each person will write about his or her group's fish and fishing trip. I will give you paper that is shaped like a fish's tail. You can write on that. When everyone in your group has written, we will put all of the tales *(tails)* together in a fish tale book.

Let's start working on our imaginary fish now. Remember, you will need to work as a group to create your fish. This fish belongs to the whole group. I will walk around the room and help you. Let's begin!

Evaluation and Processing:
Evaluate individual student performances by using the anecdotal records. Store individual fish tales in portfolios after removing them from the bulletin board display. Process the activity with your whole class by working together to publish and display the fish tale books and sharing them with one another.

Harry, the Very Smart Fish

Harry was a very smart fish.

He read books, and he studied very hard.

The other fish swam and played,

but Harry sat on a big rock and read and read.

One day, he read a book about fishermen. The book had a picture of a fish being caught with a fishing hook. Harry knew then that fishermen used hooks to catch little fish.

Harry showed the book to his friends. Everyone looked worried.

"From now on, we will all be careful not to get near a hook," said one fish.

"Harry is a hero," said another fish.

The fish cheered, "Flip, flip, stingray!"

From that day on, all the fish knew how important it was to read.

Fish Tale Pattern

See directions on page 102.

head

Fish Tale Pattern (cont.)

Directions: Duplicate the tail pattern as many times as necessary. Once the tails have been written on, attach each group's writings (in a stack) to the fish body pattern. (See illustration). Attach the tails to the body with a brad. Each group can work together to color the fish.

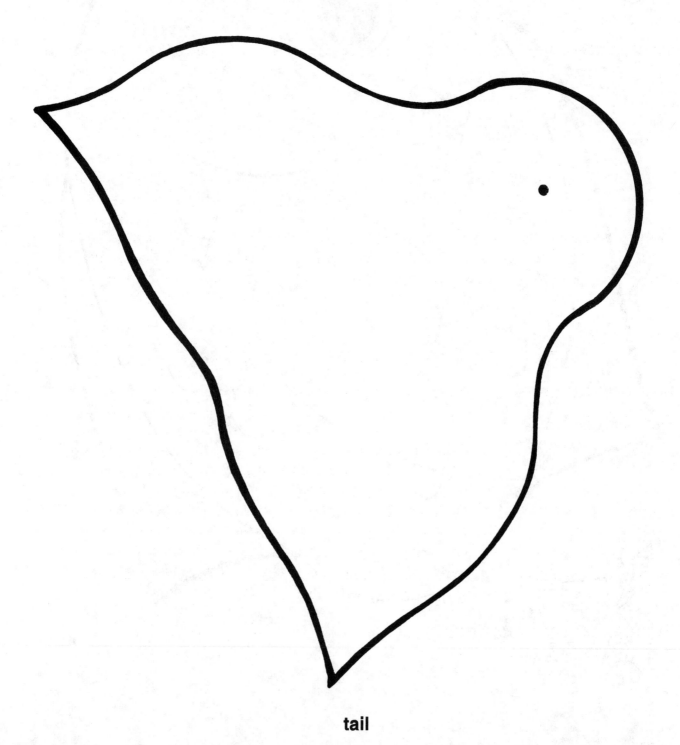

tail

Sea Pets

Purpose: To care for a sea creature and keep a written record of its progress.

Skills: writing, observation, communication, delegation, planning, cooperation, and responsibility

Materials Per Group: one fish bowl or small aquarium, goldfish (or other small, inexpensive, easy-care, freshwater creatures), aquarium supplies (such as gravel, plants, snails, and fish food), "Pet Care Journal" (page 104, several copies), "Pet Care Rules" (page 105), "About Our Pet" (page 106), and reference books about fish care

Procedures: Begin the activity by holding a class discussion about pets and their care. Ask the children to discuss their own experiences with pets.

Student groups will then work together to select, name, and care for a living fish or other water creature. Have the children meet in their groups to discuss how they want their fish bowl to look. They can then collect their materials to prepare the bowl, fill it with water, and place the fish inside.

Now, explain the procedures for taking care of the fish. Have the groups look at their "Pet Care Journal" pages and ask questions about their responsibilities. They can complete one entry for the journal every day, and they can keep all the pages in a notebook or bound together with yarn.

From the journal master page and your reference books, the class can prepare a set of rules. Post the rules in the classroom, and have each group copy a set for themselves on the "Pet Care Rules" sheet, (and place it with their journal). Remind the children of the seriousness of their responsibilities.

Finally, the groups can meet to complete the "About Our Pet" worksheet. They can share that information (and the pet) with the class. Have the groups share weekly about their pets.

To Simplify: Have one aquarium or goldfish bowl for the entire class. Have the groups work together on their journals. Rotate caretaking responsibilities among groups on a weekly basis.

To Expand: Have students make a narrated video of their fish for Open House.

Teacher Script:

Today, we are going to start a really fun activity. Each group is going to take care of its own goldfish. But before we start, let's talk about the pets that you have had. Has anyone here ever had a dog? A cat? How about a fish? Let's talk about some important things to remember about our new fish pets. What will they need to live and be healthy? Let's think of ideas, and I will write them on the board for us to look at. *(Discuss.)*

Now, let's work together in our groups to get our aquariums ready. I will help you.

Now that our fish aquariums are ready, we will plan how to take care of the fish and their homes. We will keep a record so that we know how our fish are doing over time.

Evaluation and Processing: Evaluate individual student performances by using the anecdotal records. Then process with your class by having the groups report on their fish.

Group name_____

Pet Care Journal

Pet Name _____Date_____

1. Did we feed our pet?

    Yes   **No**

2. Did we clean our fish bowl?

    Yes   **No**

3. What did our pet look like today?

    (Draw a picture.)

Pet Name _____Date_____

1. Did we feed our pet?

    Yes   **No**

2. Did we clean our fish bowl?

    Yes   **No**

3. What did our pet look like today?

    (Draw a picture.)

Pet Care Rules

Here is what we will do to take care of our pet:

1. _____

2. _____

3. _____

4. _____

5. _____

Group name_____

About Our Pet

1. Our pet's name is _____ .

2. This is how we describe our pet.

_____

_____

_____

_____

3. This is what our pet looks like.

4. Here is what we will do to take care of our pet.

_____

_____

_____

Beachcomber Puppet Show

Purpose: To create beach-related stick puppets and use them for a dramatic puppet play.

Skills: oral language, decision making, and team work

Materials Per Group: "Beachcomber Puppets" (pages 108-110), "Harry Awards" (page 111), popsicle sticks, glue or tape, crayons, felt pens, art supplies, a beige or white bedsheet, and a table or student desk

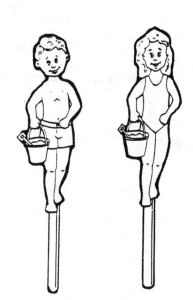

Procedures: Students will work together to make beachcomber stick puppets and plan and present a puppet show to the rest of the class. Begin the activity by introducing children to the concept of puppet shows. Some teachers may have existing puppets in the classroom. Others will choose to model the activity with pre-made examples of the beachcomber puppets. Explain that each person will make a puppet, and they must all decide who will have which puppet and what their play will be about.

Have the children sit in their cooperative groups to work on their puppets. While they are doing this, they can talk over ideas about their puppet show. Together, they will prepare a script. Then, give them class time to practice their puppet shows. Some teachers will want to have a parent helper for each group to streamline the process.

Finish the activity with puppet show presentations. Have an award ceremony to give "Harry" awards to all the participants.

To Simplify: Have children use prepared stick puppets to plan and present a puppet show.

To Expand: Have students present their puppet shows at an assembly for parents or for other classes in the school.

Teacher Script:

Today we are going to prepare for a puppet show. But before we start our activity, let's talk a little bit about puppets and why we like them so much. *(Class discusses.)*

Now, I am going to show you examples of the puppets we are going to make. As I show you the puppets, please tell me what or who they are.

These puppets are very easy to make. *(Models process.)* What I would like you to do in your groups is to decide who will make each puppet. Then, while you are working on your puppets, talk about a puppet show that you can do with them. When your puppets are ready, make up your puppet show. Practice your puppet show, and when you're ready, you will perform them in front of the class. I will walk around the room to help you. Let's begin!

Evaluation and Processing:
Evaluate individual student performances by using the anecdotal records. Process the activity by holding class puppet show presentations and by presenting each participant with a "Harry" award for achievement.

Beachcomber Puppets

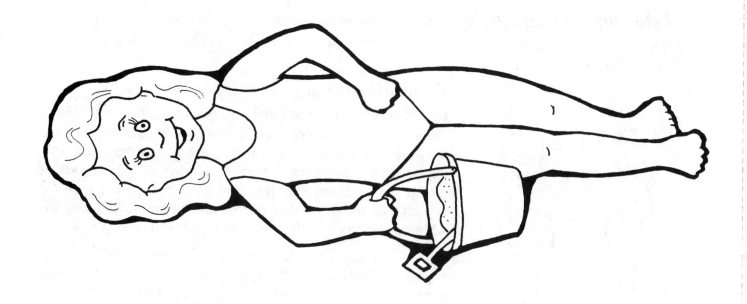

girl

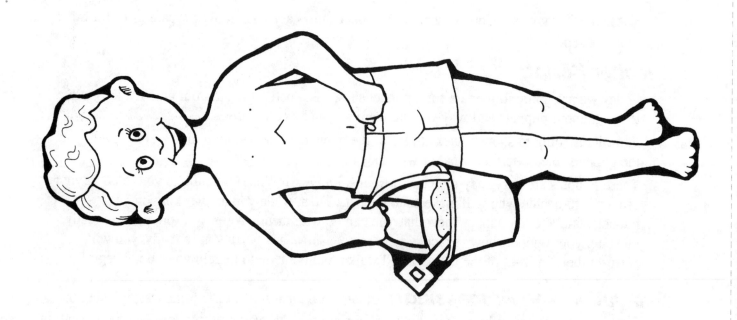

boy

Beachcomber Puppets (cont.)

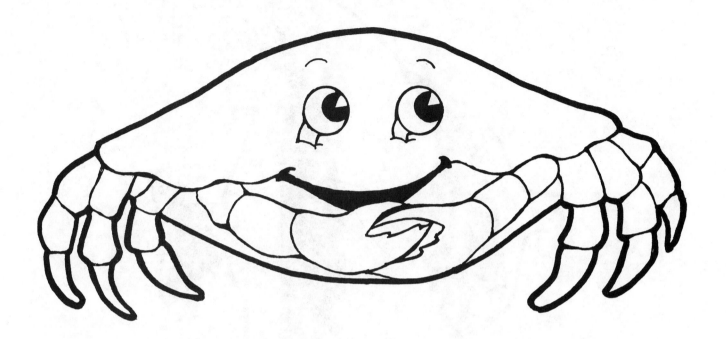

crab

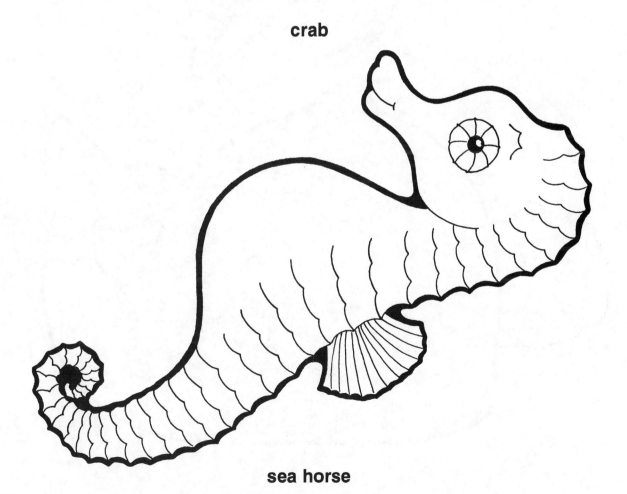

sea horse

Beachcomber Puppets (cont.)

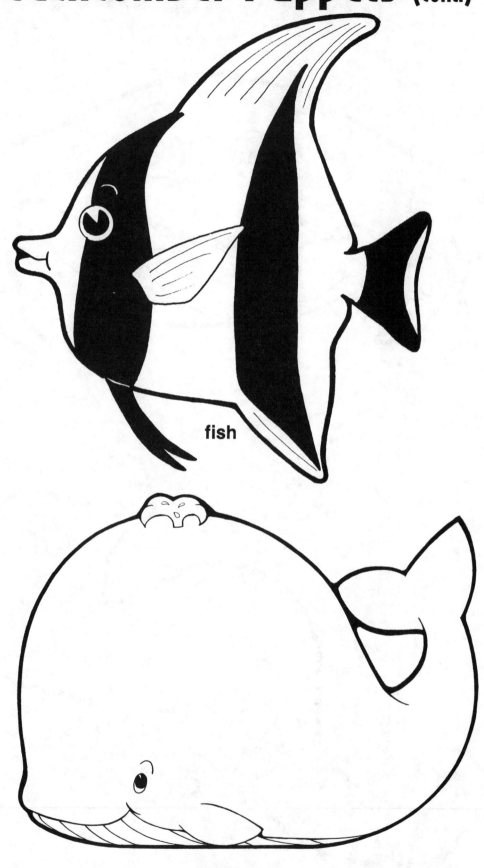

fish

whale

Harry Awards

Make-Believe Sea Transportation

Purpose: To create a make-believe form of sea transportation and explain it to the class.

Skills: team work, discussion, art, decision making, and oral and written language skills

Materials Per Group: "Sea Transportation Patterns" (pages 114-115), and assorted art supplies and materials for building transportation models (or poster paper and art supplies to draw and color the design)

Procedures: Begin this activity by recapping the various modes of sea transportation that have been studied in the classroom so far. Ask the children to share what they have learned about rowboats, sailboats, cruise ships, freighters, and so on. Then ask them to think about what kind of make-believe sea transportation they would invent if they could create anything they wanted to, no matter how strange or impossible it seemed.

Have the students move into their groups, and with the help of any available student or parent volunteers, they can talk about the kind of sea transportation they would invent if they could make anything they wanted. Use the "Planning Worksheet" to make notes.

Next, have each group sketch the imaginary transportation it designed. The groups can then write a brief description of the transportation and what makes it special.

Finally, ask the groups to build a small model of their design (or have them draw and color it in detail on the poster paper). When the project is complete, each group can choose a member to explain the transportation design to the class.

To Simplify: Have the groups simply discuss and sketch their imaginary form of sea transportation.

To Expand: Have each group prepare its form of sea transportation based on the patterns provided on pages 114-115. They can use their imaginations to put some or all of the pieces together in an interesting way. Afterwards, they can explain their mode of transportation to the class.

Make-Believe Sea Transportation (cont.)

Teacher Script:

Today, we are going to talk about all the different kinds of sea transportation we have learned about. Let's see if we can name them all. I'll write them on the board as you say them so that we can all look at them. *(Do so. Also, discuss the various features of each mode of transportation.)*

Now, let's get ready to be creative and use our imaginations! Today, we are going to work in groups to design a make-believe sea transportation. Who can tell me what I mean by "make-believe"? *(Listen and discuss.)*

So, we all understand "make-believe." Now, I want you to think about what kind of sea transportation you would make if you could make anything you want. Let your imaginations go. Don't worry if it seems too strange or impossible.

Let's get together in our groups to brainstorm for an imaginary form of sea transportation. Make notes on the worksheet I will give you. I'll walk around the room to help. After you have thought about your transportation, sketch it on the other sheet I will give you.

When your sketch is complete, your group will build a small model of it using these materials. *(Or, each group will draw and color the design on this poster paper.)* Afterwards, each group will share its design with the other groups. One person can volunteer to tell the class about it.

Evaluation and Processing: Evaluate this activity by using the anecdotal records and spending time with each group to watch its imaginative process. Be sure to make notes on each individual student's form, and date these for the portfolios. Also, use this form to note presentation skills.

Sea Transportation Patterns

Directions: Use the pattern pieces here and on page 115 for the expansion activity (page 112).

Sea Transportation Patterns (cont.)

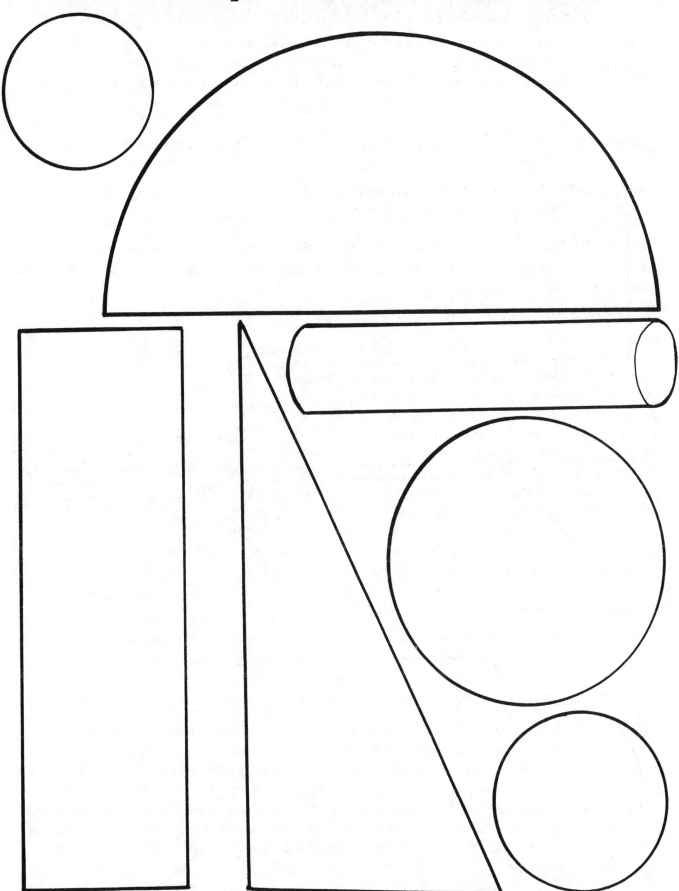

Setting the Scene: Air Mural

(**Note:** This activity completes the mural begun on pages 34-44 and continued on pages 71-77. Its process is now very familiar to the students. You may want to let them complete it as an extra-time activity. Depending on their grade level, they can work with little or no help in small groups or with partners.)

Purpose: To introduce and enhance both whole-class and cooperative group skills while building an air travel vocabulary.

Skills: word identification, reading comprehension, writing of upper and lower case letters, oral communication (both speaking and listening), decision making, and art

Materials for the Class: mural already established (pages 34 and 71), drawing paper, pre-cut strips for labels, old magazines, pencils, markers and other coloring materials, scissors, staplers, and "Air Travel Pictures" (pages 118-124)

Procedures: Begin the activity with a whole-class discussion in which students think of and name various kinds of air transportation, while you write the words on the chalkboard. Be sure to include the modes of transportation included on pages 118-124. When students are ready to go meet with their cooperative groups, assign one or more types of transportation to each group. Students work together to draw (or use the provided pictures), color, and cut out examples of their type(s) of transportation, mounting them on the air section of the mural and labeling them. They may use the words you wrote on the board during the whole-group discussion to verify their spelling. If possible, have each group work with an older student or parent volunteer.

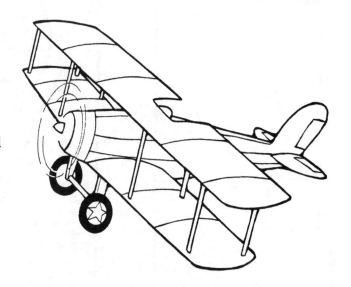

To Simplify: For pre-cooperative learners, provide pictures cut from magazines or from pages 118-124 and pre-made labels. Have students work in their groups to match the pictures and labels. When all agree that the pictures and labels are correctly matched, students may mount them on the mural. Older students and parent volunteers will be very helpful here.

To Expand: After advanced students have finished their pictures and labels and have mounted them on the mural, they may continue to work on their travel dictionaries. These dictionaries can be kept in notebooks or on sheets of paper fastened together with brads or yarn. (See "Travel Dictionary" on page 37.) Each page should have a letter of the alphabet at the top. Students will write travel words on the appropriate pages and use them as a spelling help for their writing activities. Students who want to may add definitions and illustrations. These dictionaries will be ongoing through the year, and they can be stored in the students' portfolios and then displayed during a culminating activity party or as part of an open house event.

Setting the Scene: Air Mural (cont.)

Teacher Script:

Today, we are going to talk some more about transportation. We will meet first as a large group and then move into our cooperative learning groups.

Look at the bulletin board. We will be working on the next part of our mural. Today, we will talk about air travel. Raise your hand as soon as you think of a way to travel through the air. *(Teacher accepts all suggestions and prints the words on the chalkboard.)* If that list names every kind of air travel you can think of, we are ready for the next part of the activity.

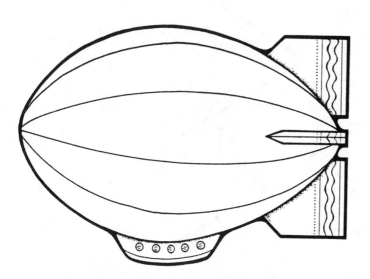

Each small group will have a kind of air travel for its own. Some of you may need to do more than one kind. *(Teacher makes assignments.)* You can color the pictures that I will give you, cut pictures out of magazines, or draw your own. Talk to the other members of your group to plan what you are doing. When your pictures are finished, you will take a strip of paper *(teacher displays)* and write the name of your pictures on it. Then you will put your picture and its name in a good place on the mural. The parent or student aide in your group can help you, if you need help. I will walk around the room to help and to answer questions.

Evaluation and Processing: Evaluate this activity by spending time with each group, listening to its discussion, and watching its creation of a product. Have copies of the anecdotal records and make notes to put in each student's portfolio. Process with the whole class by looking at and admiring the mural. Have students tell what they liked best about the activity and what they would still like to do. Allow interested, motivated students to add to the mural as an extra-credit homework assignment.

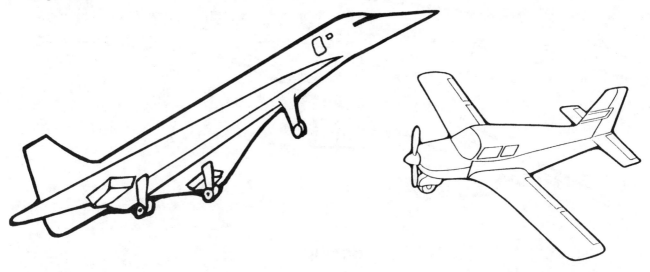

Air Travel Pictures

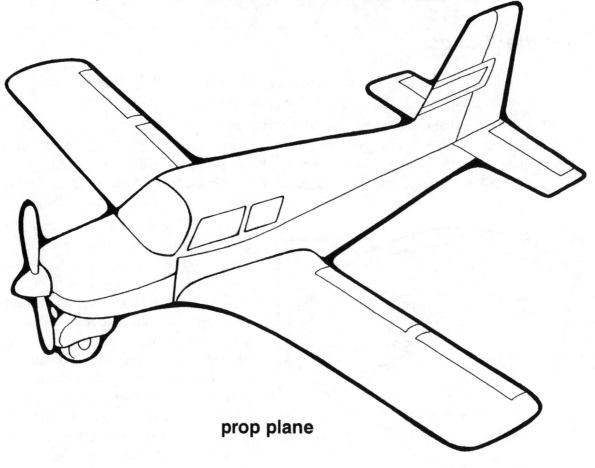

prop plane

Boeing

Air Travel Pictures (cont.)

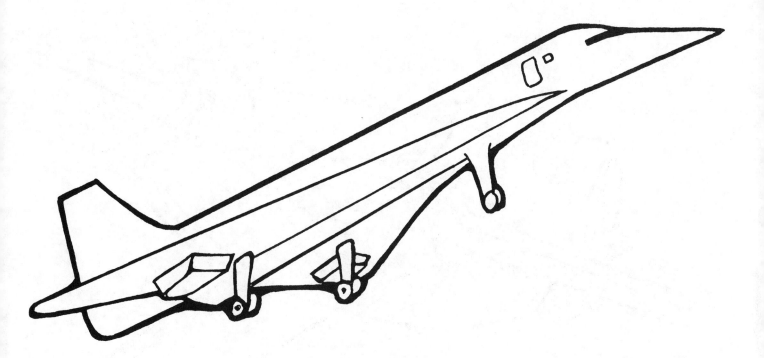

Concorde

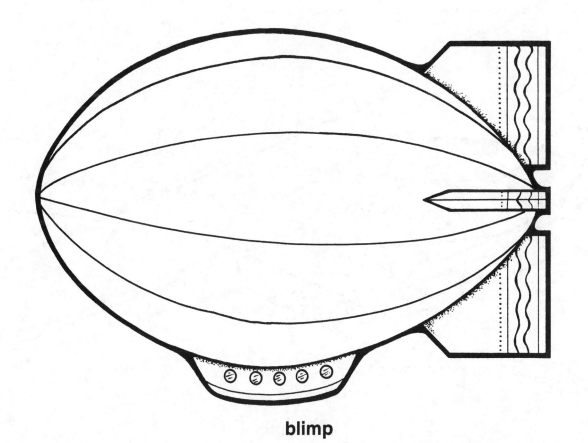

blimp

Air Travel Pictures (cont.)

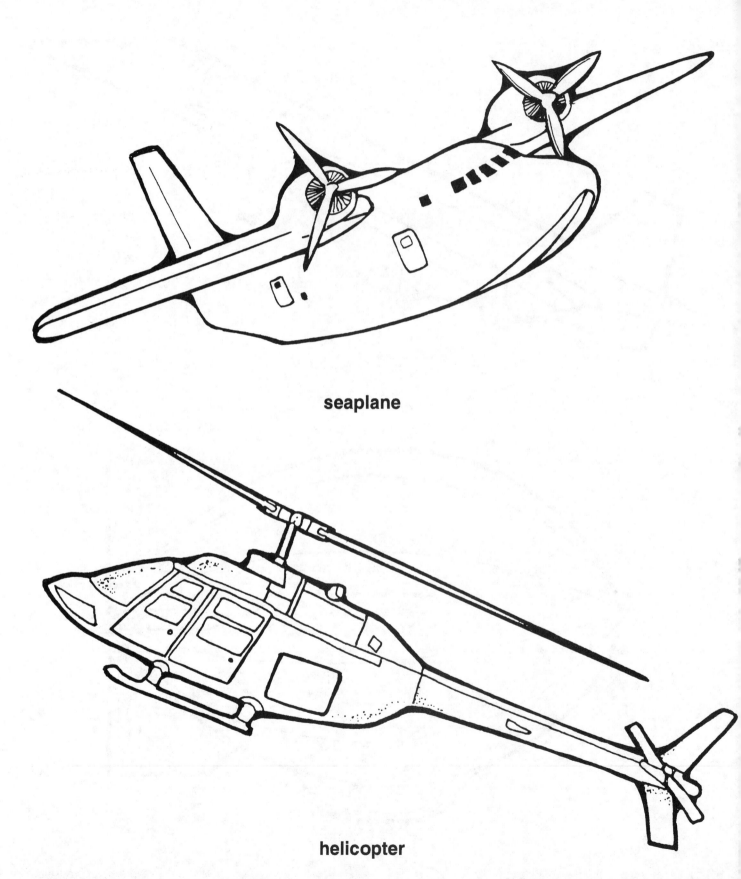

seaplane

helicopter

Air Travel Pictures (cont.)

ultralight plane

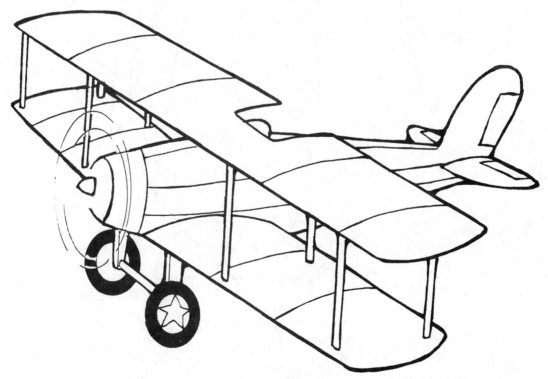

bi-plane

Air Travel Pictures (cont.)

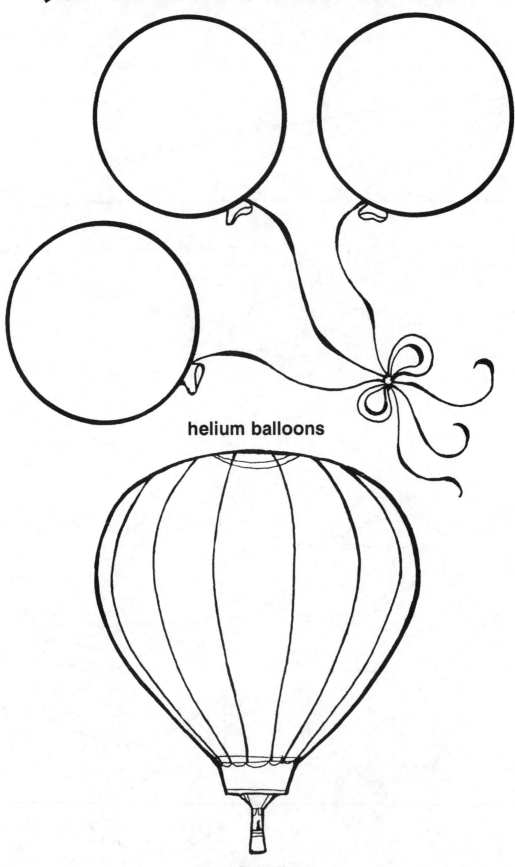

helium balloons

hot air balloon

Air Travel Pictures (cont.)

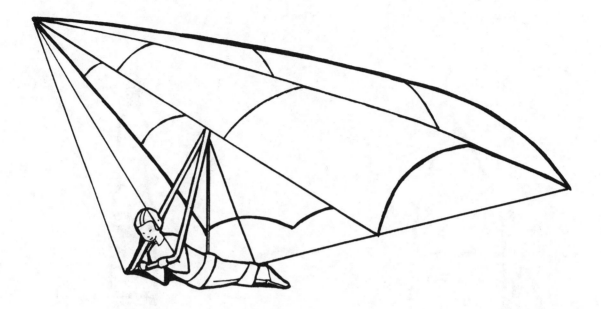

hang glider

parachute

Air Travel Pictures (cont.)

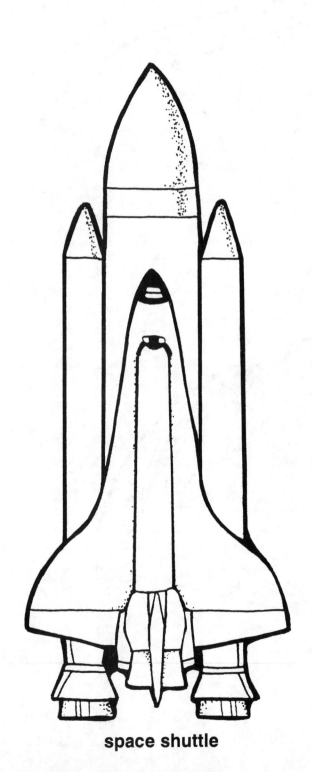

space shuttle   **rocket ship**

The Writing Process

This section of the book consists of cooperative activities designed to take the primary learner through the steps of the writing process. Although these steps may be given a variety of names, they are generally considered to follow this sequence:

1. **Establishing a need to write**
2. **Brainstorming**
3. **Organizing ideas**
4. **Writing a first draft**
5. **Editing**
6. **Revising/Rewriting**
7. **Publishing**

This process of writing differs from the traditional method of teaching writing in three notable ways. First, the writing process can stop at any point. The students or the teacher can say, "I've gotten what I need for this piece. I'll leave it at this point." Second, students are not expected to produce "perfect" examples of their writing for grading purposes when what they are really doing is producing a first-draft essay for which they had no time to prepare. Third, students are encouraged to learn that writing is a process and to be patient with themselves, to stretch their skills, and to take pride in improving their own work.

The writing process is a "real life" approach to teaching students how to write. It replicates the way people really use writing daily as a life skill and a creative tool.

People who "really" write begin by having a practical or creative need to write. They make notes as ideas occur to them. They may have an intensive private brainstorming session to start their process. Then they look at their notes or brainstormed list. They choose, prioritize, and organize them. They put their first draft on paper. If they have time, they may put this draft away for some time to take a fresh look at later. Then they edit. They may ask someone to proof their work. Only after all of this does the writer attempt a final draft. Even this draft may need more revision, perhaps for clarity, or for the addition of concrete examples.

In the classroom, the student writer can follow this very same process. In so doing, it is helpful for the children to know the following things. The editing step may occur many times and may take the form of self-editing, peer-editing, teacher-editing, and so on. Revising is a response to editing and is the option of the writer. Rewriting, or making a final draft, is fairly standard because even the most accomplished professional writer rarely produces a perfect first draft. And finally, publishing has come to mean any way of making a piece of writing available to people other than the writer.

A collection of "publishing" ideas and a list of magazines that really publish children's writing are provided on pages 143 and 144.

If I Could Fly: Establishing the Need to Write

Purpose: To motivate students to put their ideas about air travel into written form.

Skills: reading, writing, listening, thinking, speaking, and following directions

Materials Per Group: fact and fantasy books about flight, paper, drawing materials, and "Flying Machine" (page 127, one per student)

Procedures: Begin the activity in a whole-class group by telling students some of the history of flight. Over the period of a few days to a week, read aloud some books that tell about the human desire to fly, including myths as well as real attempts, both practical and impractical. Show them pictures of contraptions people have made to help them fly. Give the students plenty of opportunity to discuss all these ideas.

In small groups, have the students make plans for their own "flying machine." They should draw a picture of this machine and decide on answers to the questions found on page 127. When they have completed this part of the activity, they should each—without telling the other members of the group—begin to think of a way to finish this sentence: "If I could fly . . . ."

To Simplify: Pre-cooperative learners can draw pictures of flying machines.

To Expand: Advanced students can read at home more stories about flight and then share what they have learned with their group or the class.

Teacher Script: Today we are going to learn about how people have always wanted to fly and the ways they have tried to do that. Some of these stories are myths, and some are real. Some of the real ones are the most amazing! *(Teacher reads aloud as time permits, continuing the activity over the period of a few days to a week and encouraging discussion of each story.)*

As we have seen, people have invented many machines to help them fly. Today we will look at some of these and talk about them. *(Teacher shows pictures. Class discusses.)*

When you go to your small groups, you may keep talking about these ideas. Then, as a group, decide on an idea to create your own flying machine. Draw a picture of this machine and decide on answers to the questions found on the "Flying Machine" worksheet. Be ready to share them with the class.

When you have done all of these things, each individual should begin to think secretly of a way to finish this sentence: "If I could fly . . . ." Don't tell anyone else how you have chosen to complete it.

Evaluation and Processing: Evaluate the process of this activity and the products.

Make any appropriate notes on the anecdotal records. Process with groups by having them share their flying machine pictures and worksheet answers with the class. Remind students to keep thinking secretly about how they would complete the sentence, "If I could fly . . . ."

Group name_____

Flying Machine

Name of the flying machine:_____

How is it powered?

_____

_____

_____

_____

_____

How is it different from other flying machines we have seen?

_____

_____

_____

_____

_____

Why do we think it will work?

_____

_____

_____

_____

If I Could Fly: Brainstorming

Purpose: To generate ideas for writing.

Skills: listening, speaking, thinking, writing, following directions, and working in a group

Materials Per Group: "Brainstorming Forms" (pages 129-130) and writing materials

Procedures: This is a good small-group activity if you have an aide or parent volunteer who can remember to accept each suggestion, no matter how wild or how dull, in a nonjudgmental manner. Remind students not to tell their own secret answer for the sentence, "If I could fly . . .," but to suggest all of the ideas that came to them while they were thinking about it. Have a student secretary write the ideas on the "Brainstorming Form" (page 129). If this is too hard, the aide or parent volunteer can jot them down and help the student secretary put them on the form when the session is over.

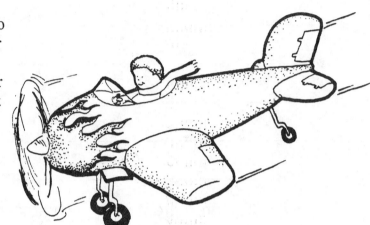

To Simplify: Pre-cooperative learners can brainstorm if a helper guides the session and writes down their ideas.

To Expand: Advanced students can have fun alphabetizing the list of ideas if they finish the activity early.

Teacher Script:

Today we are going to brainstorm in our small groups. You will all have helpers to assist you, and I will walk around to answer questions. Later we will share our ideas with the whole class. Remember, when you brainstorm, you are not judging the ideas. The only ideas that are not acceptable are things that are not appropriate for school. Do not tell your own secret answer for the sentence, "If I could fly . . . ." Instead, you can suggest all the ideas that came to you while you were thinking about it. Choose a student secretary to write the ideas on the "Brainstorming Form." If this is too hard, the aide or parent volunteer can jot them down and help the student secretary put them on the form after the session. Let's begin!

Evaluation and Processing: Evaluate the brainstorming process by spending time with each small group. Make any appropriate notes on anecdotal records which can later be put in student portfolios. Process with the whole class by having groups read their lists of ideas. Choose someone to consolidate all the group lists on the whole-class list (page 130), or ask a parent helper to do it. You will want to make copies of the whole-class list for students to refer to later.

Group name_____

Small Group
Brainstorming Form

Topic: _____

_____   _____   _____

- - - - - - - - - - - - - - - -   - - - - - - - - - - - - - - - -   - - - - - - - - - - - - - - - -

_____   _____   _____

- - - - - - - - - - - - - - - -   - - - - - - - - - - - - - - - -   - - - - - - - - - - - - - - - -

_____   _____   _____

- - - - - - - - - - - - - - - -   - - - - - - - - - - - - - - - -   - - - - - - - - - - - - - - - -

_____   _____   _____

- - - - - - - - - - - - - - - -   - - - - - - - - - - - - - - - -   - - - - - - - - - - - - - - - -

_____   _____   _____

- - - - - - - - - - - - - - - -   - - - - - - - - - - - - - - - -   - - - - - - - - - - - - - - - -

_____   _____   _____

- - - - - - - - - - - - - - - -   - - - - - - - - - - - - - - - -   - - - - - - - - - - - - - - - -

_____   _____   _____

Whole Group Brainstorming Form

Topic: _____

If I Could Fly: Organizing

Purpose: To teach students a method for organizing their ideas before writing.

Skills: reading, writing, listening, thinking, speaking, and following directions

Materials Per Group: "Clustering Form" (page 132) and writing materials

Procedures: Begin the activity in a whole-class group by telling students that they will be learning how to cluster, a way to organize ideas before writing. Copy the skeleton of the "Clustering Form" on the chalkboard and fill in the middle box with a topic. Ask the students to read this topic. Then, ask them to generate ideas to go in the ovals. Use this sample for suggestions if they get stuck.

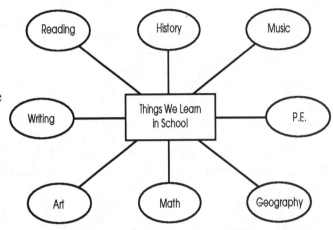

Assign a topic and have students go to their cooperative groups. They should use page 132 to cluster their ideas about their subject.

To Simplify: Pre-cooperative learners can continue to work with a helper who fills in a cluster on the chalkboard.

To Expand: Advanced students can complete several clusters on given topics or ones they choose themselves.

Teacher Script:

Today we are going to learn and practice a way to organize ideas before starting to write. It is called "clustering," and it is a very useful thing to know. Once you know how to do it, you can use it by yourself whenever you want.

Look at the clustering skeleton I have drawn on the chalkboard. The middle box holds the topic. Can someone read it for us? Good. Now let's think up ideas to go in the ovals around the edges. The things we put in there will be things that are part of this topic. Who has an idea? You are really good at this!

I'm going to erase the words we put in this skeleton form and write a new topic in the box. When you go to your cooperative groups, use the blank forms you will find on the tables. First, copy the new topic, and then cluster your ideas about it. Talk each idea over in your group before you write it on the form.

Evaluation and Processing: Evaluate this activity by spending time with each group and by looking at their completed forms. Make any appropriate notes on the anecdotal records which can later be put in the student portfolios. Process with the whole class by having group representatives read their clusters aloud. Pass out more forms and tell the students they can cluster their secret ideas about the sentence "If I could fly . . . ." They should do this for homework and have it ready for the next activity.

Clustering Form

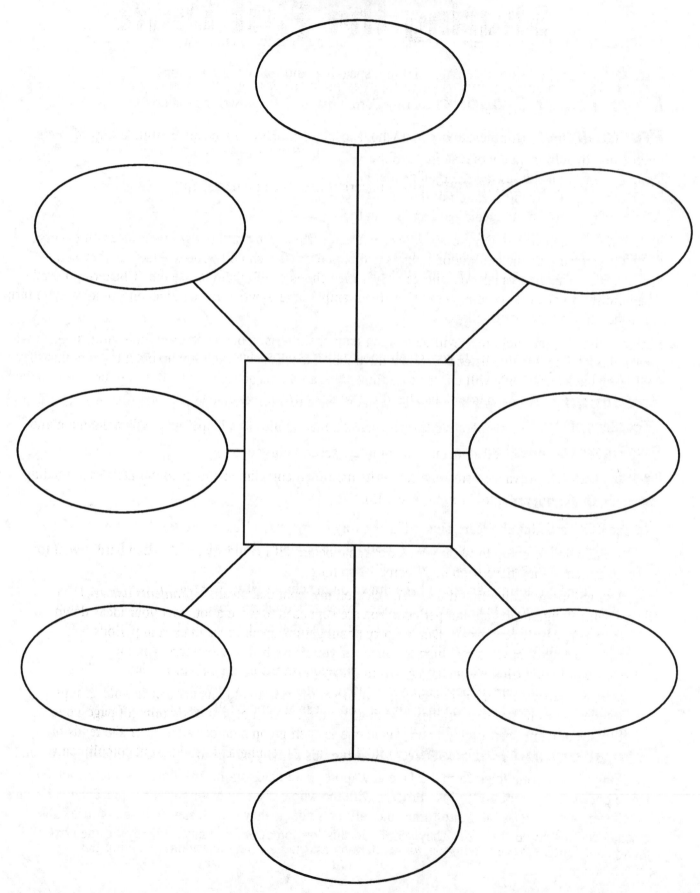

If I Could Fly: Writing and Sharing the First Draft

Purpose: To give students the opportunity to put their ideas on paper and to share them with a positive, receptive audience.

Skills: reading, writing, listening, thinking, speaking, expressing a positive attitude toward peers, following directions, and working in a group

Materials Per Student: writing materials and "Compliments" (page 134)

Procedures: Have the students write the first draft of their story that begins, "If I could fly . . . ." Remind them that first drafts are not supposed to be perfect. They should get their ideas on paper without worrying about spelling or capitals and periods. They should write as much as they can, because they can always take out things later if they choose. Tell them to use the "Clustering Form" they did for homework to help them. Give them ample time to write and an independent activity to turn to if they finish before the others.

Later in the day, tell them they will be reading their first drafts to one another in their groups. Remind them about being positive listeners. Show them the "Compliment" page, and explain to them that they will each have one. They will cut the compliments apart and hand them to their group members as the stories are read. The teacher will also hand out compliment slips.

To Simplify: Pre-cooperative learners can tell their stories to a helper who will write them and help the students read them.

To Expand: Advanced students can write their own compliments to hand out after each reading. Use the "Compliment Letter" form (page 135).

Teacher Script:

Today you are going to write your stories that begin, "If I could fly . . . ." I can hardly wait to hear them—they have been kept secret for so long.

You will be writing a first draft. Who can tell me what that means? *(Students answer.)* Right. Rough drafts are not perfect. You are supposed to write a lot. Get your ideas down on paper. Use your cluster. Don't worry about getting spelling, capitals, and periods just right. You will have lots of time to finish. If you finish before the others, you may . . . . *(Assign an independent activity to turn to if they finish before the others.)*

(Later in the day) You are now going to read your first drafts to one another in your groups. Remember to be positive listeners. I am going to give each of you a compliment page now. Please cut them apart on the lines. Hand one to each group member after he or she reads his or her story. I will also be walking around the room listening and handing out compliments myself.

Evaluation and Processing: Evaluate this activity by spending time with each group

listening to the stories. Make any appropriate notes on the anecdotal records which later can be put in student portfolios. Process with the whole class by asking how they felt about receiving the compliments.

Compliments

Great Idea!	**Wow!**
Nice Job!	**You are a good writer!**
I like your story!	**You really worked hard!**
Super!	**Neat!**
You should be proud!	**Terrific!**

Compliment Letters

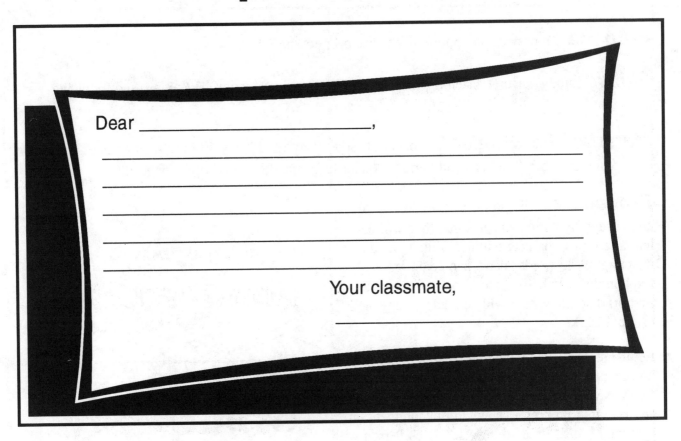

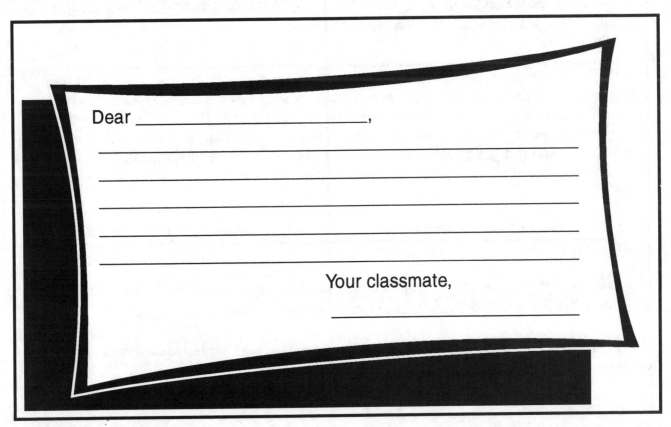

If I Could Fly: Peer Editing

Purpose: To provide an opportunity to use peer editing.

Skills: reading, writing, listening, thinking (analysis and evaluation), speaking, and following directions

Materials Per Student: copies of first drafts (page 133), a different-color pen or pencil for each group member, "Capitals and Periods" (page 138), and "Spelling Tips" (page 139)

Procedures: Begin the activity in a whole-class group by telling students that they will be learning how to do peer editing. Talk about the meaning of the words "peer" and "editing." Explain that you have made a copy of everyone's first draft so no writing will be made on anyone's original work.

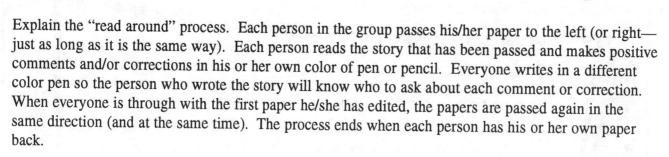

Let the students know that there is only one focus during a peer editing session. In the first session, students will look at capitals and periods as they are used in sentences. They will not comment on spelling or ideas or anything else. Each person will have the "Capitals and Periods" sheet to help this process. In the second session, students will look at spelling only. The sheet entitled "Spelling Tips" will help with that.

Explain the "read around" process. Each person in the group passes his/her paper to the left (or right—just as long as it is the same way). Each person reads the story that has been passed and makes positive comments and/or corrections in his or her own color of pen or pencil. Everyone writes in a different color pen so the person who wrote the story will know who to ask about each comment or correction. When everyone is through with the first paper he/she has edited, the papers are passed again in the same direction (and at the same time). The process ends when each person has his or her own paper back.

Immediately following, or at another time (depending on the class' ability to focus), read around again to check for spelling.

To Simplify: Pre-cooperative learners can try this process with a partner (and a parent volunteer to help). This activity will be valuable at this stage only as an introduction to the process.

To Expand: Advanced beginners can discuss and evaluate the suggested corrections and decide whether or not to make changes.

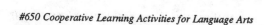

If I Could Fly: Peer Editing (cont.)

Teacher Script:

Today we will do peer editing. There is a lot to learn, but we will be doing it often so you will have a chance to practice a lot, too. What is a "peer"? Yes, your peer is someone who is your equal. Your classmates are your peers. What is "editing"? Right. Editing is making corrections on written copy. However, no one will be writing on your original first draft. I have made copies of everyone's first draft so no one's original work will be written on.

When we do peer editing, we use the "read around" process. Each person in the group passes his paper to the left (or right—just as long as it is the same way). Each person reads the story that has been passed and makes positive comments and/or corrections in his or her own color of pen or pencil. Everyone writes in a different color pen so the person who wrote the story will know who to ask about each comment or correction. When everyone is through with the first paper, pass the papers the same way again at the same time. Edit the next paper, and so on. The process ends when each person has his or her own paper back.

There is only one focus during a peer editing session. In this session, you will look at capitals and periods as they are used in sentences. You will not comment on spelling or ideas or anything else. Each person will have a worksheet that will help this process. I will walk around to help and answer questions. Let's begin. *(Do the read around.)*

Now, let's read around once more, this time looking only for spelling. Use the page I gave you to help you. *(Do the read around once more.)*

Evaluation and Processing: Evaluate this activity by spending time with each group and by looking at the editing comments each student is making. Make any appropriate notes on the anecdotal records. Process with the whole class by having students comment on the way they felt while having other students edit their work and while they edited the work of others.

Capitals and Periods

The easiest way to tell where capitals and periods go is to read the words aloud. Put the period where your voice naturally stops. The next word starts with a capital letter.

Wrong: The dog ran down the street the cat ran after him.

Right: The dog ran down the street. The cat ran after him.

Wrong: My family's favorite show is on tonight we always watch it.

Right: My family's favorite show is on tonight. We always watch it.

Even in the middle of a sentence, a person's name always begins with a capital, and the pronoun "I" is always a capital, too.

Wrong: She walked to school with mario and pham.

Right: She walked to school with Mario and Pham.

Wrong: They told me that i made the basketball team.

Right: They told me that I made the basketball team.

Spelling Tips

When you are spelling a word, you can

...sound it out.

...find it in the room.

...ask somebody.

...find it in a story book.

...look it up in a dictionary.

When you are editing another person's spelling, you can

...circle the words that do not look right.

...write the word the way you think it should be spelled.

...help the person to look up the word.

If I Could Fly: Publishing the Final Draft

Purpose: To take a writing project through to completion.

Skills: reading, writing, listening, creativity, art, thinking (analysis and evaluation), following directions, and working in a group

Materials Per Student: "If I Could Fly . . ." story, writing materials, a variety of art materials, and "Fun Publishing Ideas" (pages 141-143)

Procedures: Begin the activity by telling the students that they may now write the final draft of their stories and decide how they want to publish them. Suggest and show many different ideas for publication. Rearrange the groups to reflect the kind of publishing they want to do: binding into books at this table, pop-up illustrations at that table, writer's showcase bulletin board at still another, and so forth.

To Simplify: Pre-cooperative learners can illustrate a story that an aide or the teacher has helped them to write.

To Expand: Advanced students can enter their stories in a computer and print them out (or simply type them) and send them off to a publisher or a writing contest. See page 144, "Real Markets for Student Writing," for ideas.

Teacher Script:

Today you may write the final draft of your stories and decide how you want to publish them. Start by writing them in your final form, taking into consideration any corrections and/or revisions you may want to make.

(Later in the day) There are many different ways to publish your work. Read over these ideas and let's talk about them. *(Class discusses.)* We will rearrange our groups to reflect the kind of publishing you want to do: binding into books at this table, pop-up illustrations at that table, writer's showcase bulletin board at still another *(and so on)*. Let's gather our materials and begin.

Evaluation and Processing: Evaluate this activity by spending time with each group and making suggestions. Collect all drafts for the portfolios, along with any appropriate notes on the anecdotal record forms. Process with the whole class by discussing the procedures taken.

Fun Publishing Ideas: Book Binding

1. Stack all the pages of the book in a neat pile.

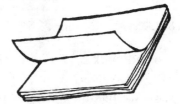

2. Place a blank sheet of paper on the top and bottom of the pages.

3. Leaving about a ½" (1.25 cm) border, staple or sew all the pages together on the left side.

4. Place two pieces of lightweight cardboard side by side. (Cereal boxes work well.) Pieces should be ½" to 1" (1.25 cm to 2.5 cm) larger than the size of the pages in the book.

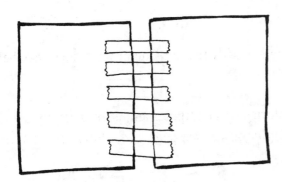

5. Leaving about 1" (2.5 cm) between them, tape the cardboard pieces together.

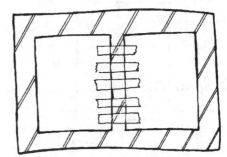

6. Put the cardboard on top of the inside of a covering material, such as fabric, wallpaper, contact paper, or wrapping paper. Glue the cardboard and covering material together, leaving a 1" to 1 ½" (2.5 cm to 3.75 cm) material border.

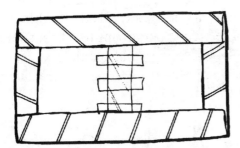

7. Fold up the edges of material over the cardboard and glue in place.

8. Glue the blank pages to the inside of the cardboard covers. Your book is ready to read and share!

Fun Publishing Ideas: Pop-Up Books

1. Fold 8 ½" x 11" (21 cm x 28 cm) paper in half crosswise.

2. Measure and mark 2 ¾" (7 cm) from each side along the fold. Cut 2 ¾" (7 cm) slits at the marks.

3. Push cut area inside-out and crease to form the pop-up section.

4. Draw, color, and cut out the object to get "popped-up."

5. Glue it onto the pop-up section.

6. Glue two pages back-to-back, making sure the pop-up section is free.

7. Glue additional pages together, making as many pages (including pop-up pages) as you like. Be sure to include a free sheet on the front and back so that those pages can be glued to a cover.

8. Glue a cover over the entire book.

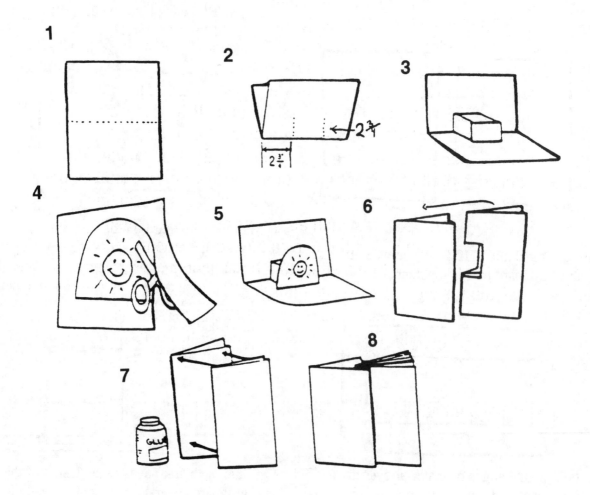

Fun Publishing Ideas (cont.)

Have You Ever...

worn it on a t-shirt?...asked to tack it to a community bulletin board?...phoned it to your grandparent?...served it on a platter?...sung it with a guitar?...framed it?...read it aloud?...had it published in a parents' newsletter?... written it in watercolor?...taped it as a radio program?...sent it to a local newspaper?...bound it in a book?...hung it in your room?...performed it for an assembly?...written it in fresh snow?...read it in a poetry parade?...sent it to a nursing home?...read it over the school's public address system?...written it in a cookbook?...received permission to draw it on a graffiti mural?...sent it to a sick classmate?...written it to a pen pal?...told it to a pet?...presented it in an animated film or comic strip?...written it in chalk on your driveway?...made a poster of it?...entered it in a contest?...flown it across the room in a paper airplane?...stitched it on fabric?...written it on an original calendar you have tried to sell?...performed it in a puppet show?...bound it and placed it in the library?...sent it in a letter to a published author?...made it a message in a bottle?...written it in sand?...sent it to a political figure, such as your mayor, congressional representative, or the President?...performed it as a skit in the shopping mall?...submitted it to a magazine?...read it to a school employee, such as the principal's secretary or a cafeteria worker?...written it in marker on a poster board?...mailed it to a former teacher?...saved it in a time capsule for the future?...sent it in a class mailbox?...illustrated it for a Valentine?...read it to the class?...included it on a writer's showcase bulletin board?...tucked it away to be read and enjoyed when you are older?

Real Markets for Student Writing

Student writing can be sent to the following addresses. Check your professional journals for more sources.

Children's Playmate (ages 5-8)

P.O. Box 567B

Indianapolis, Indiana 46206

Cricket (ages 6-12)

Cricket League

P.O. Box 300

Peru, Illinois 61354

Ebony Jr! (ages 6-12)

820 S. Michigan Avenue

Chicago, Illinois 60605

Flying Pencil Press (ages 8-14)

P.O. Box 7667

Elgin, Illinois 60121

Highlights for Children (ages 2-11)

803 Church Street

Honesdale, Pennsylvania 18431

Jack and Jill (ages 8-12)

P.O. Box 567B

Indianapolis, Indiana 46206

Stone Soup (ages 5-14)

P.O. Box 83

Santa Cruz, California 95063

National Written and Illustrated by...

(This is an awards contest for students in all grade levels. Write for rules and guidelines.)

Landmark Editions, Inc.

P.O. Box 4469

Kansas City, Missouri 64127